The Psychotherapy of the Elderly Self

HYMAN L. MUSLIN, M.D.

Professor of Psychiatry
University of Illinois at Chicago

BRUNNER/MAZEL Publishers • NEW YORK

Library of Congress Cataloging-in-Publication Data
Muslin, Hyman L.
The psychotherapy of the elderly self / Hyman L. Muslin.
  p. cm.
Includes bibliographical references and index.
ISBN 0-87630-657-1
1. Psychotherapy for the aged. 2. Aged—Psychology. I. Title.
[DNLM: 1. Psychotherapy—in old age. WT 150 M987p]
RC480.54.M87 1992
618.97'68914—dc20
DNLM/DLC
for Library of Congress   91-43419
                                                                              CIP

Published by
BRUNNER/MAZEL, INC.
19 Union Square West
New York, New York 10003

Manufactured in the United States of America

10 9 8 7 6 5 4 3 2 1

This book is dedicated to Harry Muslin, Rose Muslin, and Bernard Muslin, all of blessed memory.

Acknowledgments of committed service and support are due to Ms. Barbara Edwards, a devoted secretary and friend, and members of our Geriatric Psychiatry workshop at the Department of Psychiatry at Illinois, especially Shirley Clarke and Marcus Wigutow.

Contents

Foreword

Our concepts of age and aging are changing. Although aging is stereotypically seen as a decremental, degenerative process, we are beginning to understand that development continues throughout adult life and that each era of the life brings new demands, new opportunities, and new ways of integrating experience. The great challenge of therapy with the aged goes beyond support, beyond palliation to a recognition of the untapped potential of the person, to a freeing of that potential. Dr. Muslin sets his task clearly before the reader, to demonstrate that therapy, including psychoanalysis, has an important role in relieving suffering and promoting growth in the elderly.

How are we to understand the extraordinary variation in the elderly, the great range of responses to changes stemming from retirement, family evolution, aging, and changes in function? Our language, our constructs are not yet rich enough to separate out the impact of age itself, variations in physiologic changes, the impact of losses on the self, and the devastation of disease and dying on the capacity to function and on our perceptions of the elderly person. There is no single, coherent, easily defined group that makes up the elderly!

Among the elderly we find persons who are vital and active, who are poor and desperately needy, who are misused and abused. Some maintain roles that are centrally important in their families and communities. Many are medically ill and/or disabled. Significant numbers live in institutional settings and yet, as Boskin (1986) has noted, most of them are in fairly good health, and, compared to prior generations, their economic status is significantly improved. "So startling is the dramatic improvement in the well-being of the average elderly person, and so poorly has this information been disseminated, that misconceptions abound. . . . The other remarkable fact about the elderly population is the substantial decline in their labor force participation. Combined with the enormous increase in life expectancy, this has created a large increase in the average length of retirement" (Boskin, 1986).

We do not know how to consider retirement. Is it a reward for years of service or a shelf on which we place the used up detritus of our society? We don't know what to expect or how to think about many competent well functioning elderly who are retired. However, we do know that with the extraordinary growth in the number of the aged, the cost of health care has dramatically risen. With that rise, substantial attention has been addressed to policy focused upon costs: Costs of medical care and of long-term care; the over 1.5 million in nursing homes. Too little attention has been given to issues of disability and dependency. Even less attention has been directed to issues of adult development and continued "normal behavior" in the aging. Yet, for most of the elderly, the important issues are how to live comfortably and well in new circumstances; how to enjoy retirement; how to establish new relationships to family—to spouse, children, extended family.

Daniel Levinson (1978) has developed a theory of adult development that postulates alternating periods of transition and life structure development during the seasons or eras of the life cycle. He describes an early adult season (age 17 to 45), a season of middle adulthood (age 40 to 65), and late adulthood (age 60 to 85). In addition, Levinson (1991) has recently begun considering the dimensions of another era in development, that of late, late adulthood beginning about age 80.

Levinson describes the period of late adulthood as being characterized by some degree of physical decline and a developing sense of one's aging and mortality. One lives in a world in which colleagues, friends, and loved ones have increased episodes of illness, and in which death becomes more immediate. Societal images of appropriate role suggest that retirement occur, and that individuals relinquish authority and power to younger individuals. The central role of work in the lives of many, and its centrality to feelings of self worth must be replaced. Levinson (1976) notes that our society has failed to develop age-appropriate environments for many in late adulthood. And, he notes that for each of the greats such as Picasso, Yeats, Verdi, Freud, Jung, Benjamin Franklin, Einstein, and Sophocles, whose work flourished in late adulthood, and others far less well known who remain productive in communities, organizations, and families, there are countless others who struggle with small success to find an appropriate and meaningful place.

Can the elderly find meaning and purpose in their lives? Is continued individuation and growth possible? Dr. Muslin convincingly answers yes to these questions. His theoretical framework is that of self-psychology and he makes this theory understandable and available to therapists. It provides a base for understanding his diagnostic procedures and clinical interventions. Within this framework, Dr. Muslin identifies issues that the therapist needs to keep in mind in order to provide care empathically to the elderly. Attention needs to be paid to a range of issues: issues of slowing; of loss of function—of dysfunction and disease; of arthritis, dermatologic conditions, cardiac problems; and to the impact of stressors including perceived loss of function and loss of loved ones; and to economic strain.

Judith Rodin (1986) has pointed to the interaction of a sense of control with one's health status among the elderly. Much in the life of the elderly limits their ability to assert meaningful control. Medical care generally reduces patient control, particularly care that minimizes patient involvement in decision making. Psychotherapy helps reestablish control and, by extension, general health. One of the most gratifying therapies in which I participated was of a woman who had terminal cancer. She sought treatment in order to maintain control over her life during a period of time when family, physicians, and friends were advocating aggressive treatment with only very limited chance of effectiveness, and with serious side effects. She wished to maintain a sense of self as a vital person and was able to do so over the course of a year of living while dealing with dying. She remained a vital part of her family until her death and participated actively in her own medical care. The work of therapy is ever the relief of suffering, the enhancement of functioning, and when possible, the unfolding of one's potential.

Dr. Muslin has written a book that is a celebration of the self. With this understanding, clinicians can better help patients to deal with the processes of change in aging, to celebrate their accomplishments, to accept necessary dependence, and to avoid maladaptive behaviors.

— BORIS ASTRACHAN, M.D.

Professor and Head, Department of Psychiatry
University of Illinois College of Medicine

Introduction

LOWERING THE AGE BARRIER TO PSYCHOTHERAPY

Writing an introduction to a psychoanalytic text on a subject so dear to my heart brings a warm glow of pleasure. It revives the exciting time in the early 60s when, under the leadership of Marty Berezin, seven Boston psychoanalysts came together to share their experiences in psychotherapy with the elderly. As a result of these rather small but remarkably fertile meetings aimed at lowering the barriers to psychotherapy for the increasingly aging population, the Boston Society for Gerontological Psychiatry was born. Within a few years, *The Journal of Gerontological Psychiatry* appeared in order to carry this message to our colleagues within and without our field. Soon therapists all over the country were sharing our enthusiasm and being rewarded by the unique countertransference satisfactions Dr. Muslin addresses so well within these pages.

In our day-to-day practice, we had gradually learned that Freud's midlife pessimistic evaluation of rigidity as a precluding indicator for psychoanalysis of those over fifty was a premature conclusion even if appropriate considering the techniques available then. By contrast, we had found that many of our elder patients seemed better described as resilient as they progressively adapted to the inevitable shattering of some or all of the basic anchorages of life. Those with a significant other fared better. Other elders, increasingly stressed by the passage of time, if widowed or isolated, seemed to deteriorate more rapidly. We knew little then of the deleterious effects of bereavement upon the immune system. It was clear, however, that aging is always associated with a less intact biological substructure as it is programmed with a genetic "mean time to failure" type of code. Yet there were others, like Freud himself, who seemed undaunted by multiple confrontations with disappointments, depletion, disaster, and repeated losses. We found, as did many other open-minded therapists, that to the very end of life, some were capable of incredible feats of restitution as threats to cohesiveness, wholeness, and ongoingness in self or in self-others mounted.

In his own later years, burdened with constant pain and facing certain death, Freud left us a beautiful illustration of his life-affirming adaption by the ironic but incredibly perceptive observation, "Seven organs are competing for the honor of ending my life . . . I must hurry against the inexorable chronos." (Schur, 1972)

Erikson's profound and clear life-span studies gave much encouragement to the application of psychodynamic therapy to patients "facing not being at all" (Erikson, 1959). It became increasingly documented that not only were the elderly amenable to psychotherapy, but they, like most other age cohorts, could make excellent use of it within their family and without. Surprisingly, all "pioneers" discovered the elderly were among the most grateful and rewarding of patients with whom to work. Over subsequent years, many analysts of different persuasions reported not only successful psychotherapy, but full psychoanalyses in the last third of life (Pollock, 1987; Sandler, 1978).

In the mid-70s, I read Kohut for the first time. Fascinated by his concepts, especially as they were illustrated by Mr. Z, e.g., "It hurts when one is not given what one assumes is one's due," I wrote to express my appreciation for his recognition of the importance of the father in the development of the child. We corresponded about the resonance between my theories of midlife depletion and his concept of the enfeebled self—both rooted in empathic derailment, and certainly not representing a psychophysiological truth of old age.

He wrote back: "I found your response . . . more reassuring to me than the comprehension of my work by those who are in close contact with me. It told me a message that I all too often do not receive, that the printed word on which I must rely in the long run can truly be communicative."

In the best of self-psychological analytic written tradition, Dr. Muslin sets out to prove his case with clinical material. The uniqueness and strength in this particular approach is derived from two sources. Its uniqueness comes from its extensive interweaving of everyday problems of the elderly with an intimate and extensive Kohutian background. Its strength comes from the depth of the author's clinical experience. How simple but lucid are his words describing one of the major roots of midlife gerontophobia: "The elderly carry the message of the eventual fate awaiting us all!" How much more meaningful the news of our avoiding the imagery reflected back to us by those in the last third of life becomes when contrasted with or juxtaposed against that mirrored back by the young.

Dr. Muslin's experience reaffirms that helping and comforting one's forebears offers revitalizing rewards for therapists at different points in their life. This book joins a select few on psychotherapy of the later years that have appeared in recent decades. It carries a special message of hope of a mature clinician "to encourage psychotherapists to accept older patients for psychotherapy of all types without regarding age alone as an impediment." Accordingly, he advocates wisely, "Psychotherapy is psychotherapy for all ages."

—STANLEY H. CATH, M.D.

The Psychotherapy
of the Elderly Self

1

A Definition
of the
Elderly Self

Descriptions of the elderly commonly deal with them
as a group of people who are affected by their altered
physiology; their lack of power in social, economic, and
professional spheres; and their closeness to death.
Those who are viewed as elderly would perhaps add to
the definition that older people are among those ab-
horred in almost all human cultures and in all times.
Other groups who are similarly regarded are women,
people who are ill or are congenitally defective, and
various racial and ethnic groups (Butler, 1970; Erikson,
1982; Gutman, 1987; De Beauvoir, 1972). The abhor-
rence and ostracism turn on either such groups' behavioral or physiognomic differences from the main stream,
their real or putative power, or their afflictions (Sophocles, 1942).

The elderly would further add to the definition of
their state that caretaking is easy to dispense but difficult to obtain. Thus Shakespeare's drama in which the
aged King Lear does not receive the succor he needs

from his favorite daughter, Cordelia, is replayed again and again in families in which the transition to becoming a caretaker to one's former caretaker often is not easily accomplished or is not accomplished at all (Zola, 1972; Muslin, 1981). The psychologist would note here that while changes inevitably do take place in the aging soma and psyche, there is no *one* elderly self—thus implying that the various structures of the self do not react to the ubiquitous alterations and stress in a simple reflexive manner. Just as no two nervous systems are alike in their resistance to aging, so no two selves are alike in their response to their changes in their roles and vigor; some selves with abundant endogenous stores of self-worth and self-calming mechanisms respond to aging quite differently than do those whose entire source of approval is linked to minute-to-minute activities representing achievement.

The following are some of the factors commonly identified with the *elderly*.

1. As a group, the elderly are people going through the physiological and metabolic processes of aging so that their functioning has become altered or impaired.

2. As a group, the elderly are those persons whom their cultures have designated as unable to continue as participants in the professional or business world. This definition ordinarily includes a numerical standard for aging, such as beyond age 65 or beyond age 70.

3. The elderly are those persons whose aging processes have advanced to the level of impaired functioning of various systems of the body or mind and so they are, therefore, simply awaiting their death.

4. The elderly are those persons whose physiological and metabolic aging processes have advanced to the level of diminished functioning so that they no longer are capable of living independently, and so require supervised care.

Thus the definition of the elderly requires the input of a variety of points of view: the cultural, the sociological, the economic, and the biophysiological. And most observers would hasten to add the psychological view, since there are some persons in their ninth, and even tenth decades who have just begun to demonstrate a significant negative alteration in their soma and psyche (Muslin & Epstein, 1980; Busse & Pfeiffer, 1972; Berezin & Cath, 1965).

In response to these alterations in the soma, there are, as in the adolescent, intrapsychic changes necessary for the adaptation of those undergoing the profound social and organic changes of aging. And just as in adolescence (a so-called phase of development also with physiological and cultural aspects that was unrecognized as a developmental phase before the 20th century), there are those elderly persons who will go to their deaths without ever experiencing the profound physiological changes of aging or significant intrapsychic alterations (Riesman, 1954; Zinberg & Kaufman, 1963).

What are the psychological alterations in the elderly that constitute an adaptation rather than an adjustment to the oft-present somatic and sociocultural changes? What constitutes the completed modal self of the elderly, if such exists? Is there a justification for designating the time before death as a specific phase of somatocultural-psychological change through which all humans will pass?

Perhaps the overview pertaining to the elderly that the psychotherapist could accept includes the following: (1)The various institutions of the culture and the family for persons in the seventh decade and thereafter impose limitations on functioning. (2) The deterioration in the organs and musculoskeletal systems and the behaviors that derive from these alterations proceed at a variable, and sometimes accelerated rate in persons in their 70s and beyond. (3) There are a variety of intrapsychic reactions to the sociocultural standards and somatic changes—or expectations—imposed on aging persons, some of which constitute adaptive changes and others that do not. The fact of the psychological reactions to aging is unequivocal, but the nature of the reactions is, of course, idiosyncratic. They include affect imbalances, such as sadness or hypomanic affects, to anxiety reactions ranging from nervousness to panic and neurosis, and expressions of hostility ranging from bitterness to rage and homicidal fantasies.

From the vantage points of the foregoing observations, there is justification for describing people undergoing the aging process as belonging to a defined group, albeit one so defined by society. Deterioration—its changes and the psychological reactions to it—is a natural progression, but the "traditional" roles assigned to the elderly are not necessarily dictated by nature. These cultural impositions on aging persons also result in significant psychological reactions on the part of the victims—from adaptation to painful depression to fragmentation of the self.

THE LINES OF DEVELOPMENT OF THE ELDERLY SELF

The *elderly self* is a composite of the intrapsychic alterations of the different agencies (structures) of the mind. In this form, it will reflect the accents of a particular culture with regard to aging, deterioration, and death, in addition to the other variables noted previously—the rate of somatic deterioration and the capacities of a particular individual to change. Thus the elderly self must be defined in cultural and biopsychological contexts. It is, therefore, imperative that the psychotherapist be aware of what the particular surround expects of and offers its aging (the sociological input) as well as of the impact of aging on the person's capacities for action and thought (the psychological experiences).

A composite definition of the elderly self is as follows:

The elderly self is the self of aging people that has become altered in all or many of its structures and functions in reaction to a constellation of societal and biological influences that reflect a particular society's views of an aging person, as well as the individual biological givens. An *elderly self* is a self that has passed through specific alterations in its self structures that have evolved in reaction to the specific internal and external milieus. A cohesive elderly self is one in which the self-alterations have resulted in an adaptive self without the symptoms and signs of excessive reactions to the external world in the form of loss of worth or self-fragmentation and its vicissitudes as evidenced in neurosis or psychosis.

The crystallization of these self-changes in reaction to the sometimes malevolent, sometimes benevolent forces of nature and nurture that we are defining as the self of the aging are sufficiently prominent in all cultures that we can speak of *the elderly self* as an entity by which to measure one's aging patients. The entire self of the *aging person* undergoes these alterations in becoming an *elderly self* in each of its agencies: the sense of reality; the pole of ambitions; the defenses against drives; the value system (the pole of values) and, therefore, the quality and quantity of shame and guilt; the strength and quality of drives; and the attachments to other selves as either objects or selfobjects (Neugarten, Havighurst & Tobin, 1968).

The completed elderly self is a self that is adaptive to its milieu—not just as an adjustive self, implying acceptance of its inadequacy. Further, it is a self that is, depending on the surroundings not only at peace with itself, but is also a joyous self reflecting achievements that are deemed laudatory (Kohut, 1977; Muslin & Epstein, 1980).

The following chapters center on the development of the cohesive elderly self* and the psychopathological conditions in the elderly, as well as the psychotherapies that are helpful to them.

---

*For those readers who are interested in learning more about the findings and positions of self psychology, please refer to *Psychotherapy of the Self* (Muslin & Val, 1987).

2

On the Development
of the Elderly Self

The completed elderly self is a self that has become transformed from the self of adulthood, the preceding era, with its unique values and programs of action consonant with an altered physiological status. The developmental period of aging, as do other developmental periods, necessitates self-transformations to effect the desired end stage. Changes in the pole of values, for example, are a major feature of the developmental task of becoming an adolescent. Each developmental phase—childhood, adolescence, adulthood, aging—involves specific self-transformations, in addition to the changes in physiology and physiognomy, in order for persons in that particular phase to complete the developmental task rendering them, for example, adolescents or adults. From this point of view, there are many 15-year-olds operating with an 8-year-old pole of values who will never be adolescents functionally. Similarly, there are 80-year-olds who will attempt to function as if they were in their 6th decade of life.

Also from this point of view, the person in a particular age period should be identified and labeled as adolescent or adult only if that person has been able to effect the self-transformations that meet the criteria for a particular developmental phase. Just as an adolescent is not only a 15-year-old person, so an elderly person is not just an aging person, but is an older person who has undergone major alterations in his or her self-structures that identify the person as an elderly self. The outcome of the developmental process, the cohesive elderly self, is a self that is in harmony within its components. In this cohesive elderly self, the transformed inner values that are held can be matched by the now-altered assertive forces of the self, assuring a cohesive shame-free self. Conversely, a person without the self-alterations required in any developmental period suffers the vicissitudes of a self in disarray with a loss of self-value and other features of a self in disequilibrium, such as the propensity to fragmentation. A person in the fourth decade of life who has not effected the required self-changes of an adult will not be able easily to perform the empathic tasks required of a parent or spouse, since the values and standards of a responsible caretaker have not been formed. Such persons will compete with their children for the ministrations of their spouses or be unavailable to the children since they cannot empathize with the needs of their wards for *their* input. Their self-transformations have not resulted in a self-experience as a calmer and soother of the young.

Thus in every developmental period, there are those unfortunates who have not been able to effect the changes that would afford them the gratifications of being, for example, an adolescent or an adult (cf. Chapter 3).

In their passage to becoming an elderly self, there are

those throughout history who have loudly proclaimed the grief attendant on being aged without being aware that they have not been able to alter their selves in accordance with the requirements of a cohesive elderly self. Horace, Ovid, and Juvenal exemplify the description of the aged as those ancients for whom life ceases with the advancement of age. Horace wrote, "Sad age come, farewell to laughing, happy love and easy sleep" (De Beauvoir, 1972, p. 121). Ovid observed, "Time, O great destroyer and envious old age, together you bring all things to ruin" (De Beauvoir, 1972, p. 122). And Juvenal complained, "What a train of woes—and such woes—comes with a prolonged old age. To begin with, this deformed, hideous, unrecognizable face; this vile leather instead of skin; these pendulous cheeks; these wrinkles . . . The ancient no longer has his wits. A perpetual train of losses, incessant mourning and old age dressed in black, surrounded by everlasting sadness—that is the price of a long life" (De Beauvoir, 1972, p. 123).

In the 16th and 17th centuries, Shakespeare wrote of his fears of the ravages of time. In *As You Like It*, he described the aging man in this fashion:

The sixth age shifts
Into the lean and slippered
pantaloon . . . . and his big manly voice,
Turning again toward childish treble, pipes
And whistles in his sound. Last scene of all,
That ends this strange eventful history,
Is second childishness and mere oblivion,
Sans teeth, sans eyes, sans taste, sans everything.

(Act II, sc. VII, 1, 158-164)

And Lear, crying out against old age and disloyal children:

You see me here, you gods, a poor old man,
As full of grief as age; wretched in both,
If it be you that stir these daughters' hearts
Against their father, fool me not so much
To bear it tamely; touch me with noble anger
And let not woman's weapons, water-drop,
Stain my man's cheeks!
(Act II, sc. IV, 1, 276-321)

In the 18th century, Swift presented an unusually despairing picture of aging in *Gulliver's Travels* (Chapter 10), when he described the *Struldbruggs* or Immortals. These were persons in the Luggnoggian kingdom who were destined to be immortal and were recognized at birth by a red spot over their left eyebrow. "When they came to fourscore years . . . they had not only all the follies and infirmities of other old men, but many more which arose from the dreadful prospect of never dying" (p. 127). Swift alluded to the notion of life as "perpetuity of youth, health and vigour," and thus the awfulness, to him, of immortality as an older person (Swift, 1952).

In the 20th century, perhaps no one has captured the despair in those whose conception of old age as deterioration without any gratifications as has the playwright Samuel Beckett. The old people in *End Game* (Beckett, 1947), communicating from one garbage can to another, can only speak of their past as sources of empathy and tenderness, with the present (old age) likened to a garbage can and they to the garbage.

The completed elderly self—the self that has been mobilized to alter its functioning in reaction to the biosociological stimuli impacting on the aging throughout history—shows its differences from the adult self in its several compartments. The self, as Kohut (1959) initially redefined it, is the body of experiences of which one is aware or of which one can be made aware—one's body, one's mind, one's perception of objects and selfobjects. Moreover, it refers to experiences, hitherto unknown, of which one can be made aware now and in the past. He later added to these seminal insights into the self the organizing scheme of the self called the bipolar self. The bipolar version of the self is a model of a self in which a pole of ambitions—the assertive strivings—is conceptualized, which through its talents and skills acts to live up to its pole of values and thereby to avoid shame. The pole of values is the interiorized unconscious and conscious repository of ideals and morality codes. Some facets of this structure, which date from the first year of life, reflect the caretaker's (selfobject) collection of restraints and permissions and have become the permanent values of the self (Kohut, 1971).

While the poles of values and ambitions are an important heuristic and functional concept, they are not to be conceived of as anatomical entities residing in the left temporal lobe, for example, or in the limbic system. Neither are they to be taken as a set of neurophysiological mechanisms evoked by particular stimuli. As aging begins, the "elderly self" begins to form. Perhaps the most significant alterations in the self that initiate the evolving of the elderly self are in the standards of the self, sometimes referred to as the ideals, by which one measures oneself. An aging person, for a variety of physiological and psychosocial reasons (all "legitimate"), must alter his or her standards for what has, in the previous age periods, constituted acceptable, or even exemplary, behavior. Conversely, in those aging persons whose energy output has become diminished (or for whom the job market has shrunk or who are part of a culture that does not value the aged), but who retain standards for themselves that are not compatible with their current somatic state, the self-experience may be one of chronic "empty" depression or chronic inadequacy (Kohut, 1971; De Beauvoir, 1972).

THE POLE OF VALUES

The line of development of the so-called pole of values, one of the structures of the mind that differentiates human beings from other mammals and in its varieties of form differentiates one self from another, begins with the initial contact between the self and its original caretaker (selfobject). The caretaker's handling of the infant immediately shows the infant the value of the human encounter in relieving the child's agitation. In each caretaker–child unit, a value is laid down within the first weeks and a connection is made or a neuronal circuit is established between the touch, the rocking, the smile, and the experience of being calmed, as well as an association between the child's oral needs and its specific relief of tension at the hands of the caretaker (later to become elaborated into the desire for the human encounter to relieve tension). It is during these early months of life that significant interdictions and significant encouragements—the major elements of the value system—are laid down. The association of the entire gamut of infant behaviors with mirroring (support) or hostility determines the fate of those mental or physical acts as the mirroring or interdictions become permanent elements of the value system to stand throughout life as ideals of behavior to live up to or as acts that are forbidden. Thus the expected behaviors documented by Stern and others (Greenspan, 1981; Sanders, 1964; Stern, 1984; Tolpin, 1971) in the first year of life are met in each infant with the memories of the interdiction and acceptance reactions of the selfobjects. Therefore, "expected" behaviors, such as crying, eye contact, crawling, vocalizing, standing, stranger anxiety, and walking, can be assessed only in conjunction with the responses of the available selfobjects.

The complex mechanisms by which values are interiorized are not understood. The neurophysiological mechanisms by which perceptions become memories also await further elucidation. At this stage, what we have is evidence that the manifest data of interdictions and acceptances become "memories" and function as determinants of behavior, as well as of the cohesion of the self, by evoking particular affect states ranging from pleasure to despair. It is also not known whether specific affects are released when ideals are not lived up to (the shame equation) or injunctions are transgressed (the guilt equation) or whether a continuum of affects is evoked when behavior emerges that is in opposition to the self-values. In this hypothetical overview, shame would be the mildest form of negative experience associated with behaviors evoking displeasure and guilt would be the most intense response evoked by behavior deemed unacceptable.

After the stage of the infantile development of the self, the so-called pole of values continues to accrete standards that, through the evocation of particular affects, influence and determine behavior. Kohut's (1971) hypothesized version of the development of the pole of values, as well as other aspects of the self, following Freud (1917), was that, directly after an episode of optimal frustration (nontraumatic separation or rupture of the self/selfobject bond) of a child's desires, the child would internalize the precepts and other features of the selfobject, and thus structuralization proceeds in the pole of values, as well as in all compartments of the self. Other hypotheses that seem plausible to pursue in understanding internalizations—the pathway from perceptions to memories, that is, the formation of neuronal circuits, some of which affect future behaviors—is that perceptions may become internalized as a result of either the process of identification with an idealized selfobject and its precepts or of the process of selfobject mirroring that defines certain behaviors as laudable, acceptable, or noxious.

It has become customary to conceive of the self as becoming fixed in many of its compartments, especially the so-called pole of values, at an early age. Freud, as have all other students of the mind, recognized that certain elements of the self had established a consistency of functioning at the end of the oedipal stage (age 7)— which, he concluded, was when the major internalizations from one's selfobjects were completed. Additions and alterations to one's pole of values, however, continue throughout life, as witness the dramatic changes in the lives of certain people at different ages (Gandhi, Churchill, Hitler, Eleanor Roosevelt, Lyndon Johnson, Golda Meier—Muslin & Desai, 1985; Muslin & Jobe, 1991). These people responded to a variety of stimuli—external and internal—that resulted in changes in the standards they held for themselves as they developed beyond childhood and which determined the directions of their lives. The factors that fuel the internalization of new ideals are complex—separation, death, mirroring and the need for mirroring, and the perpetual search for ideals and idealized figures. However, as one can see from the study of leaders in all fields, the self is capable of transmutations throughout life.

THE POLE OF AMBITIONS

When Kohut described the bipolar self, he identified that sector of the self that comprises the assertive strivings that make up the pole of ambitions. The pole of ambitions comes into being as a result of the activities of the selfobject parent who serves as the medium of applause for the unfolding self. After internalization of the selfobject's confirmation, the self is permanently endowed with an experience of worth. The outpouring of self activities is similarly endowed with the affirmatory experiences of the caretaker. Thus an individual's self-worth and its motor arm, the pole of ambitions, reflect the history of the individual's self/selfobject life.

Throughout life, the self is in need of the oxygen of selfobject infusions. In adolescence, for example, the need for a mirroring selfobject parent to give credence to creative activities is time-honored. And as one continues to develop, constant selfobject refueling is necessary to promote or maintain self-worth. At times, these selfobject contacts will approach approving–admiring–calming–merging interactions resembling the archaic fusions of childhood. At other times, the support rendered will be an experience of empathic resonance—the admiration of a spouse or friend through which the adult self can experience a revival of the memory traces of the archaic selfobject's mirroring or calming and soothing, and in this manner restore a disarray that resulted from a temporary deficit in self-esteem.

In the mature cohesive self, there is an abiding need for exogenous selfobject support; no ordinary, nonpathological self can be sustained without such support, implying that endogenous stores of self-worth are never sufficient to maintain a cohesive self. Thus the capability to extract support from one's environment is an important factor in maintaining the cohesion of the self.

In adult life in many Western societies today, the adult self has a paradigm for acceptable behaviors—that of the achieving self, whether it be in art or in science, in the culture's values or overvalues, or in activity as compared with contemplativeness.

When the self is enfeebled from whatever cause, there is often—especially in those selves in whom the endogenous stores of self-worth are modest or minimal—a period of self-disarray. Thus in illness or in retirement or in the aged, the self may be vulnerable to losses or disappointments, that is, vulnerable to episodes of lowered self-regard and subsequent fragmentation.

THE PASSAGE FROM AN AGING PERSON
TO AN ELDERLY SELF

In aging people—or, more accurately, in those for whom the advancing years have been marked by illness or debilitating somatic dysfunctioning or whose culture has imposed changes on them—the self is in need of transformations in order to survive. The extent of such modifications is determined by "outside" demands and the capacity for alteration based on the individual's neuronal circuitry and psychological plasticity; that is, fixations of the self that determine the capacity to move away from ancient methods to secure gratifications and to avoid psychic injury. In those for whom the endogenous sources of mirroring and internalized ideals have never been sufficient to provide an adequate sense of worth, the admiring reactions of those around them and the external standards of the culture that one must meet to achieve the admiration are *necessary* for self-cohesion. For these persons, removal from active life during the time of aging is a ticket to despair since it is only through exhibiting certain behaviors that reflect a specific and valued role in their culture that these persons—*absent* of self-admiration and of internal ideals to follow—experience a sense of worth and the certitude and rectitude that accrue only through being fused with the ideals and idols that are valued in their society.

The significant transformations of the aging self take

place in several areas: the pole of values; the pole of ambitions; various functions of the self, such as the reality and defense functions; the emergence of previously contained drives and object and selfobject relationships; and the cosmic narcissistic changes described by Kohut—the alterations of the self as revealed in humor, attitudes toward dying, the capacity for empathy, and the acquisition of wisdom (Kohut, 1971).

The Transformation in the Pole of Values

The need of aging persons, as we have defined this term (that is, those who have been removed from or deprived of their previous way of life by becoming aged), is to alter their values or standards for themselves so as to alter their judgment of acceptable behaviors—behaviors that avoid shame and evoke mirroring. The term "alter" is used to indicate that, in some instances, the standards that have been in place as ideals to live up to in order to maintain intrapsychic cohesion must be totally discarded; in others, they require modification. A surgeon or an electrician suffering the hand tremors of Parkinson's disease cannot continue in accordance with the ideals of their particular vocations. Their standards for acceptable activities that will provide for self-cohesion must be changed since their value of mastery through action cannot be maintained by turning to some other lifelong career. In a similar fashion, a self-standard for mastery through action cannot be maintained in a person who no longer can dress unassisted or cook owing to crippling arthropathy. A forcibly retired engineer whose energies had been invested in "his" firm must now alter his standards or suffer a self-disruption of painful shame. We are not unaware that some options exist in the last type of cases; in some instances the individuals may be able to sustain their self-esteem by securing a similar position in another firm or by starting their own enterprise. Certainly, these exceptions are known in our culture.

Kohut's ideas about maintaining self-esteem in the formed self were that a person has several "programs of action" with similar sets of ambitions leading to particular sets of ideals, all in the service of maintaining self-cohesion. People, of course, differ vastly as to the importance of their different poles in determining their approach to life. There are some people whose values are a major source of initiating action; they are "led" by their ideals. There are others whose ambitions drive them to a continued quest for applause; they are "pushed" by their ambitions.

How does the process of change occur and how does it work? As aging people become permanently ill or undergo a change in their role in the culture, they must abandon their particular ideals of action or achievement and separate themselves from the standards of other life stages, which now evoke only shame, as they cannot live up to these old standards. The process of separating from one's ideals constitutes a major loss and ushers in an expectable diminution of self-supplies; for many, entering into the elderly phase of life is marked by a period of depression. This sadness at the outset of the elderly phase defines the *support* required—for a self flagging in worth—by the aging person during this transition.

The next phase in the development of the elderly self is that of reconstitution, the development of new ideals, and with it, the development of new programs for the self. The pole of values must include standards or goals for the self that are in harmony with the somatic alteration or social–cultural role alterations. They will include such standards as becoming the "overseers" in the family or in business or profession—those elderly persons who are valued for their wisdom but who do not participate in the day-to-day activities in the office, on the job, or in the home. Another standard for the reconstituted pole of values is that of becoming the embodiment of "the continuum of life." The elderly person becomes the link between one generation and the succeeding one. With each of these new standards comes a new program for the self, as the self lives up to these altered standards. Another standard for the reconstituted pole of values lies in the standard for the elderly to "be" the model for their viewing of life, its losses, and impending death in a state of equanimity based on an altered viewpoint that Kohut called "cosmic narcissism" (Kohut, 1971).

Another standard, or an acceptable model, is of the relationship between an elderly person and his or her caretaker, in which the former selfobject changes places with the self it has been leading or nurturing—the daughter or son becomes the caretaker of the parent, who becomes the entitled recipient of the care (Muslin, 1981). There is also the ideal of the aging one as the entitled seeker of purely pleasurable activities, such as travel or hobbies.

Thus the process of separation from one's former

ideals and the establishment or internalization of new ideals to serve as guides to the self are perhaps best conceptualized as the repair of a minifragmentation. When ideals no longer serve as a guide to activity that can be pursued or accomplished, the tension arc of self-action is interrupted and the self is deprived of any programs of action. Those ideals that were important in earlier epochs of life—from childhood to the time of retirement—no longer can be of service in the aging self. The need exists for the aging self to turn away from ideals that no longer can command action and to interiorize new ideals that not only will be capable of execution, but also will afford the self sufficient mirroring.

Among the abiding values that are transmitted in a particular culture and that become internalized in the self over time are those attitudes relating to the elderly—the norms for the acceptable behavior of an elderly person, as well as the respect that is to be shown to the elderly. These values are, of course, transmitted through the manifest behaviors of respect or disdain shown to the elderly and interiorized throughout the development of the self in that particular culture. They are elements of the individual's pole of values that serve as standards one can follow since they have been affirmed by the culture over the centuries. (In Chapter 3, we discuss those aging people whose standards of behavior from previous developmental periods cannot be altered and who consequently are unable to alter their values.)

In summary to this point, the pole of values in the self of the aging person becoming a genuine elderly self becomes transformed in two directions: (1) the diminution of the previous ideals that commanded action programs, and (2) the enhancement of the culturally approved standards for the elderly that are already part of one's value system and now become a major force in the transformed pole of values, and an important guide to behavior. In this manner, a self distinguished by a value system in earlier phases of life that held up ideals for achievement "at any price" becomes transformed into a self whose value system compels behavior to live up to its new standards for "spectator" activities. A final important transformation in the elderly self is that the elderly self must emphatically alter the standards for acceptance of dependency to a new standard for the acceptance of nurturance and assistance. Dependency needs are to be deemed safe, to be accepted and valued.

The Transformation in the Pole of Ambitions

The pole of ambitions of the self is the term used to describe the overall capacity for assertiveness in a self. It includes the description of the degree of neutralized or unneutralized aggression present in the self, as well as the factors pressing for the discharge of assertiveness and the frequency of such discharges. It is a useful concept, but without any claim for neuroanatomical or neurophysiological validity; it serves as a method for describing the self-ability to express affects and to create, initiate, and complete a project. An important facet of the individual pole of ambitions is the intensity of the self-need to evoke mirroring and/or the self-experience of assertiveness as a positive, or at least a safe, experience.

If the self's pole of values presents ideals of behavior for a person to live up to—including a particular form of activity such as that of an artisan or athlete—the self's reservoirs for action, the so-called pole of ambitions, is the motor force in striving to live up to the ideals of the self. There are those selves whose lives are dominated by their eternal quest to become valued or powerful; these are the mirror-hungry selves whose poles of ambitions can be said to be hypertrophic. There are those selves in whom assertiveness has always been associated with rejection and so their pole of ambitions is anemic and their assertiveness diminutive. At times, the self is able to correct its enfeeblement through compensatory grandiosity, the mechanism by which the self can overcome its enfeeblement or collapse by instigating the discharge (and, at times, massive outbursts) of ambitious or grandiose activities.

What are the transformations in the pole of ambitions in the aging self? The need to be admired does not disappear with aging. However, the available stores of energy are diminished, which, of course, influences all activity. The manner in which one's ambitiousness emerges as an aging person is altered to match the standards for what the particular aging person deems acceptable, as we have described. The wish to be applauded (the activity emanating from the pole of ambitions) emerges in a fashion that is deemed appropriate or worthy (the influence of the pole of ideals). And so King Lear's ambitions emerge in a manner characteristic of the aging self: his ambitions to receive applause are cloaked in the activity of a benevolent monarch passing on the baton of command to his three daughters, an activity that matches exactly his value of the good, retiring patriarch, the father-emeritus. In sum, the pole of ambitions of the aging self undergoes alterations in the quality and quantity of the striving for applause. Thus the need to be venerated may be deeply felt by the aging person—with the need for applause emanating from one's pole of values.

The Psychic Defenses

In the aging self, the self-defenses continue to function as important regulators of the self. And, of course, the defenses characteristic of a particular self maintain their status; they are one of the fingerprints of a self, an easily identifiable mark of a person. Perhaps the most characteristic alteration in the defenses of the aging person is the more frequent utilization of disavowal and of denial of infirmities and of impending death. For those aged persons who do talk about death, the discussion is often of an abstract nature rather than an interaction marked by the appropriate despair over the permanent separation that death brings.

When Freud (1906) discussed this time of life, he wrote that the impermanence of people or cherished values evokes a heightened sense of love and admiration for the transience of life: "Transience value is scarcity value in time" (p. 305). Kohut (1966) evolved similar notions of the "proper" attitudes toward the transience and end of life:

Man's capacity to acknowledge the finiteness of his existence and to act in accordance with this painful discovery may well be his greatest psychological achievement, despite the fact that it can often be demonstrated that a manifest acceptance of transience may go hand in hand with covert denials. (p. 454)

Goethe (1828) expressed similar views on transience in the following stanza:

And till thine this deep behest: Die to win thy being! Art thou but a dreary guest, Upon earth unseeing. (p. 6)

In contrast with Goethe, Freud, and Kohut, this author believes that their views are expressions of the mechanism of denial and disavowal that many need in the face of death. It is his view that the percept of the ultimate separation experience—death—cannot be nakedly accepted and must be denied or disavowed. And so in discussions with persons who are aging, one may hear a great deal, but not about death and dying, and ofttimes this is the way it should be.

ON THE NEED TO RECOGNIZE
THE BEHAVIORS OF THE AGING

For those who have lived or worked with aging people, their behaviors are familiar and so have become commonplace. It is important to highlight these behaviors so that they might be recognized as characteristic alterations in the aged and not confused with pathology of either an organic or functional nature.

To begin with, the manifest behaviors of the aging are commonly altered so that their words and affects at times emerge in a slower or inconsistent tempo. There may be a fairly long pause between the posing of a question and answer—perhaps because of hearing difficulties or because the aged person did not immediately comprehend what was being asked. The affective aspect of the behavior of the aged is often subdued or anergic. It is also important to recognize other aspects of the aged person's nonverbal behavior—so as to be able to differentiate between modal behavior of the aging and signs of disequilibrium.

The verbal behavior of the aged at times reveals, apart from the slowing of speech and sometimes flattening of affect, a constriction of interest that at times may shade into perseveration, or the repetition of stereotyped responses to all inquiries. Another feature of the verbal behavior of the aged can be the concretizing of the thinking processes, demonstrating a difficulty or slowness in abstracting and generalizing that results in the infrequent use of metaphors and other symbolic forms of expression.

A common feature of aged persons is a difficulty in some aspects of memory. The ability to store new percepts and to recall these percepts becomes increasingly diminished for many aged people. This difficulty results in a degree of mortification for some, in avoidance of or withdrawal from interactions with people in others, and in confabulation or lying in still others. Another adaptation by some aging persons to recent-memory deficits is the attempt to recapture the past by speaking or reading of persons from their childhood or youth.

Comprehension is another intellectual task that is difficult for many aging people, especially if it involves the manipulation of several concepts or areas of knowledge or time frames to form an understanding of the subject under scrutiny.

At times, the orientation of the aged person becomes unstable, and while the person's awareness of places and persons may be intact, his or her orientation as to the time of day or month or year may be imprecise or uncertain.

The impact of intense anxiety on the mentational processes is commonly disruptive, of course. However, in the elderly, the effect may be devastating and cause what is called a fragmentation reaction: an outpouring of anxiety mixed with confusion and other unadaptive behaviors revealing that the patient's orientation is disrupted in all spheres, and that memory and judgment are also relatively affected.

THE SELF-AS-A-WHOLE

The self-as-a-whole refers to the person's abiding total experience of himself or herself. It represents the face, voice, and behaviors one imagines are being presented to the world and that, of course, most commonly are only a version, and sometimes a distortion, of what is manifest to an observer, even an empathic one. At times during the developmental cycle, the transition from one physiological and psychological phase to another brings with it a self-experience of foreignness or unfamiliarity as one captures one's newness in a mirror. The repetitious checking with the mirror during adolescence as the soma becomes "precipitously" altered reflects an attempt to become familiar with a new self as a whole. This "phantom-limb" phenomenon—the amputee's feeling that a body part has *not* been lost, removed, or altered—can become a permanent part of the self; the person is always surprised at the mirror reflection of his or her physiognomy. In these instances, the self-as-a-whole, the percept of one's self, has never become transformed to match the actual altered self—that of the adolescent, the young adult, the obese, the chronically ill, or the dying.

And what of the self-as-a-whole in the aging person? The pervading experience of one's self-as-a-whole undergoes alterations, or remains an unshakable percept in some, as a result of one's reality as visible in reflecting surfaces or in reaction to the manner in which one is treated in a particular culture. As the evidence begins to mount that the people in one's milieu exhibit behaviors of deference and accommodation, and even veneration, simply owing to one's advancing age, the impact on one's self-as-a-whole becomes altered and the transition to another phase of development receives a strong impetus. The self-recognition that one has now entered the last or final stage of development is not always, of course, an unimpeded or unresisted percept. The phantom-limb phenomenon is omnipresent as people continually retreat in their self-percepts to their versions of their previous selves or are surprised at people's responses—the ticketseller automatically giving a senior-citizen discount without asking one's age, the young person offering a seat in the bus or train, the common inquiry as to the aging person's state of health when the gait slows, and the anxious silence that ensues when the aging person suffers a lapse in memory.

As the self-as-a-whole proceeds to its final form in the aging person, there is (often) a period of vulnerability to narcissistic injury, real or imagined, as the person accommodates to the loss of the previous self and its potential for securing the predicted positive responses from both the outside and the inside world. It is a period of self-upheaval, a minifragmentation at times, during which the predicted reactions of approval and admiration (mirroring) and other familiar or expected responses from the surround have become altered. It requires time—psychological as well as ordinary time—to experience the new self as a valued self and thereby reacquire the steady state of well-being that had been part of one's life.

During the time that the self undergoes transition in the aging period, and with it perhaps the loss of positive responses from the environment, the capacity of the milieu as a whole to function as the empathic selfobject becomes the crucial variable in the cohesion of the self. Consider the self-needs in other transitional periods, during the time of dying, for example. This a time when the elements of the self are often in need of reminders and reassurances of worth. It is a time often enough when an empathic selfobject is necessary for the survival of the self, implying that endogenous sources of self-sustenance are often inadequate to maintain a cohesive self. In these people, self death precedes tissue death by a considerable length of time (Muslin, 1981).

THE CRYSTALLIZATION OF THE ELDERLY SELF

When the alterations in the aging self have crystallized—those alterations evoked by the culture's behaviors toward the aging, the deteriorations of mind and body, or illness—the *elderly self* can be said to be formed.

The elderly self is a self that has adapted, not adjusted, to its somatic limitations. Further, it is a self that has adapted to the limitations imposed by the cultural institutions—in the family, on the job, and in the reactions of the culture toward the aging. It is a self with a particular configuration: unique values and unique ambitions that are particular to this specific group of aging or aged persons who have passed through the described stages mark the person as a member of the elderly group in the culture to which he or she belongs. The badge signifying membership in this unique group of the elderly is not age, but rather the fact that one has undergone the self-transformations that marks one as elderly as surely as any other badge of an age or of an ethnic or racial group identifies the adolescent, the Asiatic, or the Caucasian.

IN SUMMARY

The self-changes from an aging to an elderly self can be summarized as in the following.

The Behaviors in the Elderly Self

It is important to call attention to the uniqueness of the behavior in the elderly, verbal and nonverbal, so as not to pathologize behaviors that are reflective of modal changes in aging people. In verbal behaviors, for example, the tempo may be slowed and the vigor of communication diminished. There may be a paucity of responses. The affect may be diminished in general, leading the observer to assume a depression. The nonverbal behavior of the aging may be manifest in gait changes (slowdown) or in inattention to grooming.

Important aspects of the altered behaviors in the elderly are the changes in the basic functions of memory, orientation, and comprehension. The well-known alteration in their memory functions lies in their diminished ability to form new circuits and to retrieve memories, especially recent ones. Orientation to persons and places is least affected, but orientation to time is sometimes defective. Comprehension of spoken and written material is sometimes affected by a difficulty to retrieve associations to the verbal symbols and, therefore, to assign meaning.

The Pole of Values of the Elderly Self

A distinctive feature of the elderly self is the transformed value system—the ideals that serve as codes according to which people pattern their outcome. In the completed elderly self, the values transmitted by the particular culture are those identifying the elderly as persons who will, or will not, be appreciated for their prior achievements as caretakers, mentors, and standard bearers or depreciated for their here-and-now activities. The altered value system includes the value of the wise empathic symbol of continuity as a person who has come to grips with the fact of death and other losses.

The Pole of Ambitions in the Elderly Self

In the pole of ambitions of the completed elderly self, the observer can witness that this self has commonly gone through alterations in the quantity of energy release and in the form that the ambitions now take, that is, to acquire respect or even veneration as an elderly person.

The Self-as-a-Whole

The crystallized self-perception of the self-as-a-whole in the elderly is an important transformation that is necessary in the passage to the elderly self. When completed, the self-image—and, therefore, the self-expectations—is in harmony with the actual capacities of the self, without loss of self-worth and so without shame.

The next chapter will discuss psychopathology in the elderly self and present an overview of psychotherapeutic approaches for those elderly persons who require psychotherapy.

3

Psychopathology and Psychotherapy in the Elderly

In those aging persons who are not able to transform their selves into cohesive elderly selves, the *resistances* to the required self-transformations are varied. These resistances take the form of psychopathological syndromes, some of which are particular to the aging and others that are not. One such syndrome is "the resistance to aging" syndrome. Other psychopathological states in the aging are those that are specifically evoked by the reaction of the self to the external forces particular to the aging self, the so-called "emerging neuroses of the elderly." There are also psychopathological states that represent patients with character disorders and neuroses that have continued into the elderly years (Gitelson, 1948; Goldfarb, 1955; Mechanic, 1972; Muslin & Epstein, 1980; Neugarten, 1964; Neugarten, Havighurst, & Tobin, 1968; Roth, 1976).

RESISTANCE TO FORMING THE ELDERLY SELF

Resistance to the formation of the elderly self is found in those for whom the prospect of having had to retreat from their ordinary methods of adapting to life has brought about disarray. Shakespeare's story of King Lear describes an aging parent who suffers a precipitous loss of esteem when he can no longer command. Shakespeare sets the tone of the tragedy from the outset; the king demands of his daughters that they profess their admiration for him precisely when he gives up the baton of command (Muslin, 1981). This resistance-to-aging syndrome is a reflection of those selves whose endogenous sources of worth are limited and who, therefore, over a lifetime, have relied on their ability to evoke the needed responses by their actions. The mirror-hungry, the acquisitive personality, and the clamorer all describe this self, victimized by the inner hunger that is never satiated since the striving for applause is the unconscious outpouring of an unrecognized infant who is clamoring for the reliving of the *actual* scene with the archaic selfobject mirror. Those aging persons who are fixated onto their previous selves might be described as having an "adult character fixation," reflecting the inability to enter into the self-transformations that become the elderly self. Because of their fixation on their previous selves, these people—still caught up with their previous value system and ambitions—will experience intrapsychic distress when their ideals cannot be realized or their assertiveness cannot gain enough momentum to carry a project through to its end.

When the aging person with an adult character fixation finds that he or she cannot finish a project (write a law brief, finish a bookcase, repair a plumbing fixture) because his or her energy or strength has failed or the ability to synthesize complex ideas was not up to previous standards, the person experiences shame. Over time and with multiple "failures," these fixated people are at high risk for a chronic depression; to them, becoming older is truly tragic (Butler, 1963, 1975). In others in the aging group who have not moved away, intrapsychically, from their adult selves, their *perception* of their self-as-a-whole has not been altered to match their actual aging selves, with their diminished assertiveness and physical changes. When they are responded to in a manner that reveals that they are being reacted to as an aging person rather than as a love object of another age group, they experience an intense loss of self-worth. For them, becoming old also is truly tragic, without any gratifications (Blazer, 1982).

THE EMERGENCE OF NEUROSES
AND CHARACTER DISORDERS

Pathology of Self or Self Disorders

Self psychology asserts that all forms of psychopathology are derived from defects in the overall structure of the self or from distortions of the self, both of them attributable to disturbances of self/selfobject relationships in childhood. Further, self psychology asserts that, in contrast to classical analysis, the conflicts in the object-instinctual realm (i.e., in the realm of object love and object hate, in particular, the set of conflicts called the Oedipus complex) are not the cause of psychopathology, but its results (Kohut, 1977).

The self, in adult life as well as in childhood, will be in a state of cohesiveness, harmony, or fragmentation; that is, it will be enfeebled, distorted, or firm—reflecting the success or failure of the archaic self/selfobject relationships. Should there be a failure in these relationships in childhood or in adult life, certain consequences will obtain. One such consequence is the painful experience of a massive failure of the self/selfobject relationships, that of fragmentation. In the view of self psychology, fragmentation is the central pathological experience referring to a breakdown of the self. It is initiated by a massive loss of self-esteem, followed by the global anxiety referred to as disintegration anxiety. Directly after the advent of disintegration anxiety, the self is experienced as losing its cohesiveness, with the usual splitting or fragmentation of the self-functions of reality testing, memory, and orientation of space and time, and the loss of the intact experience of self-observing. The various experiences of the different organs, previously coalesced in the intact experience of the total body self, are now experienced as separate and become the foci of enhanced attention, and even of preoccupation to the point of hypochondria. Finally, a failure in a self/selfobject encounter will commonly lead to a rage reaction that is unique. These eruptions of rage, the so-called narcissistic rage reactions, are without a purpose, save to vent destructiveness on anyone in the immediate environment. It is one of the ubiquitous responses to the experience of losing control over one's selfobjects (Kohut, 1971, 1977).

A massive or chronic failure during the phases of childhood when the self is unfolding may result in a fragmentation that eventually will be resolved, that is, the self will reconstitute itself (the fragmentation will subside), but the self will not have permanent alterations. The overall experience of the self will be that of a self chronically low in energy—a self depleted of vigor and without evidence of the experience of joy. This self will be quite reactive to criticism and failures by becoming more withdrawn or caught up in the explosion of a narcissistic rage reaction that, as stated previously represents a reaction to the loss of control of the functions of the selfobject and, therefore, is without an object on which to ventilate the rage. Depending on the specific type of selfobject failures, the resulting self-distortion may be that of a self weakened in its poles of assertiveness or ideals or in the areas of its talents and skills. These defects will, of course, lead to the absence of formulated programs of action in life (in educational, athletic, or musical pursuits, for example).

The overall result of such self/selfobject failures may be a self that sees life as empty and is constantly in the throes of loneliness. This self may be quite resistant to human encounters, and although it experiences loneliness that it would like to overcome, maintains a conscious attitude of haughtiness and isolation. At times, this self may attempt to gain self-esteem support through a variety of activities designed to enhance the chronic emptiness, such as compulsive homo- or heterosexuality, bouts of addiction to substances to provide calming experiences, or compulsive episodes of stealing to enhance esteem.

At other times, the selfobject failures in childhood eventuate in what appears to be a syndrome of neurosis. These reactions occur when, after a failed selfobject encounter, such as a failure of mirroring in the oedipal phase of childhood, the child becomes preoccupied with the particular phase-specific drive or phase-specific developmental task, which ultimately leads to a fixation on the particular drive or developmental task. The failure of a self/selfobject encounter during the oedipal phase of development leads to a child's becoming permanently preoccupied with the fears of that phase in life that were never allayed (Basch, 1981; Muslin, 1985; Tolpin, 1978; Wolf, 1980). Thus an oedipal fixation or an anal fixation represents a failed self/selfobject relationship of that developmental era of childhood.

The secondary elaborations of the self breakdown at those specific times in childhood when developmental tasks needed to be mastered, with the usual addition of the selfobject functions of mirroring or guidance, are of the nature of an exaggerated attention on the drive currently in focus and on the defenses elaborated in an attempt to ameliorate or repress the exaggerated drive fragments.

To repeat, the sequence of the self-dissolution into the psychopathological forms previously outlined is as follows: The cohesive self, in response to a self/selfobject rupture, breaks down or becomes fragmented; it then may take one of several pathways. The fragmented self may maintain a state of chronic fragmentation (protracted fragmentation disorders, borderline personalities); it may repair itself without evidence of the previous state of breakdown (episodic fragmentation); it may reequilibrate itself with newly developed defenses against selfobject bonds (narcissistic personality disorders); or it will focus on the drives that are in focus as part of the current developmental phase or are activated as a manifestation of a regressive reaction (neurotic syndromes) and secondarily develop defenses against the egress of the specifically elaborated drives (Kohut, 1971, 1977).

Episodic Fragmentation Disorders

Perhaps the most common psychic disturbance in the aged is that self state that occurs after a self/selfobject breakdown. All around one's self as an aged person are losses and disappointments—losses of friends and relatives, of body and mind capacities, and of physiological well-being. Other losses and disappointments are more subtle: the interest and capacity to be involved in new music and literature, or in current politics and world events and many other areas of life that are of little interest to the aged.

Reactions to a breakdown in self/selfobject bonds are, of course, ubiquitous, since failures and disappointments in self/selfobject involvements range from those archaic self/selfobject ties that continue over time to those that are experienced as so-called mature selfobject encounters. In adults, the need to enter into an archaic self/selfobject bond is limited to those instances in which the self is subjected to psychological trauma requiring a temporary merging relationship. These are, of course, instances in which the self is suddenly devoid of narcissistic supplies and is in need of fusion with a mirroring selfobject or a revered leader. Archaic self/selfobject bonds are always in the service of investing the self with the experiences of worth, strength, and calming and soothing. In childhood, these experiences give the self the requisite strength of cohesion; in adulthood, they effect a repair to a fragmenting self when entered into temporarily in relation to the stress of dissolution. Mature selfobject encounters are those interactions in which the self is in need of a temporary enhancement of esteem, that is, self situations of esteem deficiency such as found in the innumerable states of self-doubt. Here, the self-experiences of the selfobject actually are not those of an object fused with one's self and under one's control; rather, the self has a reactivation of the early self/selfobject mergers and experiences a state of esteem enhancement, thus resulting in a repair of the self's cohesion. Seen in this way, much of adult interactional life consists of mature selfobject encounters with others who function temporarily to repair a flagging self-esteem or of symbolic encounters with music or literature in which the self is uplifted or invigorated.

Thus episodic fragmentations or near-fragmentations or simple instances of loss of esteem or threatened loss of worth are part of one's modal reactions to a complex world of victories, near-misses, and failures. In a more or less cohesive self, the repair, in most instances, will be effected by entering into a so-called mature self/selfobject encounter. In those instances where the demands for cohesion are intense, the previously cohesive self will fragment, albeit temporarily, and seek an archaic self/selfobject encounter in which a merger will be effected. For example, the psychological reactions of the person who has just been informed that her long-standing state of weakness is due to a malignancy in her colon frequently are the self-experience of fragmentation. It is to be hoped that the individual's distress will be followed by a self/selfobject merger with a trusted caretaker or relative. In these situations, the fragmentation experience is short-lived if empathic caretakers recognize the manifestations of the fragmentation and respond appropriately with a dose of mirroring or by allowing themselves to become the target of idealization (Kohut & Wolf, 1978).

Self-fragmentation resulting in neurotic syndromes

In the view of self psychology, drives come into focus when the self is fragmenting—hence the designation that drives are disintegration products of a fragmenting self (Kohut, 1977). From this vantage point, consider the self of the oedipal-phase child and his or her selfobject needs for his or her emerging phase-specific assertiveness, including sexual assertiveness of a homoerotic and heteroerotic nature (in each case, with hostility toward the opposite parent). If a situation results in which the selfobject supports are missing or inadequate and the child experiences the parents' withdrawal or rejection during this important developmental phase, the self-depletion will result in a fragmented self. The result, in some instances, will be not an eruption of the so-called narcissistic rage, but a preoccupation with the drives derailed from the now-fragmented self. In the ordinary functions of the self, the drives are a vital part of the self, seeking and maintaining contact with the world, including the world of selfobjects. In a fragmented self, the drives are in a free state and clearly visible, since they are not bound up with the functions of the cohesive self.

To return to the oedipal child whose self, now in a fragmented condition, will have unleashed "oedipal" drives, these phase-specific drives will eventuate in repetitive experiences of anxiety centering on tissue destruction—the so-called castration anxiety with its attendant features of anxiety dreams of mutilation—and the buildup of irrational guilt. Self psychology argues, in disagreement with classical psychoanalysis, that the emergence of the oedipal neurosis signifies a failure of the oedipal phase. These failures of the selfobject supports usher in a fragmentation of the self, followed by the child's repetitious preoccupation with the assertions specific to the oedipal phase and the subsequent fears and guilts. Self psychology further holds that if a child in the oedipal phase of development becomes the recipient of helpful selfobject supports, he or she will emerge from this normal phase of development with heteroerotic and homoerotic strivings with a minimum of guilt and castration. In contradistinction to classical psychoanalysis, self psychology does not regard the oedipal phase as "the pivotal point regarding the fate of the self that it is with regard to the formation of the psychic apparatus" (Kohut, 1977, p. 240).

In summary, the neurotic syndromes, which in classical psychoanalysis emerge from the predetermined unfolding of the drives coming into intense conflict with ego defenses and superego, are conceptualized in self psychology as one of the possible outcomes of a self in fragmentation. Self psychology holds that if the self is intact, no preoccupation with the drives in an isolated fashion takes place. Thus from the viewpoint of the self psychologist, although an oedipal phase of development is a ubiquitous happening, if the child receives adequate selfobject supports (mirroring and calming-soothing-directing) he/she will emerge with a firming up of assertiveness that is now more adequately controlled with a firming up of the gender experience. Contrariwise, if there has been a selfobject failure to the modal egress of assertiveness in an oedipal youngster, the derailed (unattached) instinctual drives will be seen as naked lust and hostility.

In treating the aged, the therapist occasionally sees a patient who ostensibly has developed a neurosis—an obsessive-compulsive neurosis, for example—without any history of a similar illness. After a great deal of exploration and perhaps not until much later in the therapy or analysis, the history of a previous similar neurosis will emerge. In these instances, a self-rupture will evoke a fragmentation, followed by the emergence of an archaic (childhood) self state replete with the patient's archaic (childhood) means of resolving the anxiety. The phobic measures of projection and displacement followed by avoidance represent such a solution to a fragmentation that is common in old age. Aged patients commonly become phobic about their physicians, their illness, the dark—seemingly for the first time. In obtaining a person's history, the therapist may uncover previous phobic states—old adaptive measures re-evoked by the aged person. Similarly, one sees manifestations of repression and conversion (the hysterical neurosis) or the manifestations of isolation and undoing (the obsessive-compulsive neurosis).

The Narcissistic Personality and Behavior Disorders

Self/selfobject failures during the early development of the self, when protracted, result in a variety of self disorders. Those self disorders, called the narcissistic personality disorders, and the acting-out variety of such disorder, the narcissistic behavior disorders, ordinarily result from a failure of functioning of the mirroring selfobject and an inability of the idealized parent to compensate for the primary selfobject failure (Kohut, 1977). The resultant self is one in which the cohesiveness of the total self is defective and both poles of the self are inadequately filled. This self is vulnerable to fragmentation, especially in relation to further losses of esteem from its milieu. The self-experience is commonly a reflection of the diminutive poles of assertiveness and ideals; thus the common experience is one of emptiness and/or loneliness. However, the self-needs for mirroring or leadership are commonly defended against by attitudes of haughtiness and superciliousness, reflecting the anxiety about allowing any further selfobject encounters to transpire.

Another common experience in persons with these disorders is that they become immersed in transitory relationships in which an archaic self/selfobject dyad is formed and then rejected, ordinarily out of a mixture of anticipated psychic pain and disappointment since the

relationship cannot offer the longed-for childhood gratification. Fragmentation states commonly lead to intense
loss of esteem, the so-called empty depression, that is,
without prominent guilt. Another common feature of
the fragmentation states is the experience of disintegration anxiety—an anxiety state marked by panicky feelings, dissociations, and end-of-the-world sensations
—followed by mentational dysfunctioning (memory
loss, reality-testing deficits, loss of synthesizing, and
the appearance of derailing of associations) and hypochondriasis. The hypochondriasis in fragmentation
states reflects the state of the "unglued" self.

While the ordinary experience of a single organ or
anatomical part is minimal in a cohesive self, when the
self is fragmenting, a particular organ percept now functionally split off from the rest of the self may suddenly
be experienced in a highly charged fashion. A patient
in the middle of a fragmentation reaction may complain
of unusual body feelings and localize them to an awareness that the face or nose or abdomen is now viewed
quite differently: it seems too large, too prominent.
These experiences reflect the body percepts becoming
split off and, for the first time, prominent in the patient's awareness. Patients with narcissistic personality
disorders sometimes exhibit behaviors that express their
reactions to insult or their needs for calming and soothing or mirroring. These narcissistic behavior disorders
include the behaviors of the compulsive homosexual, of
the addict, and of delinquents who steal as a symbolic
expression of the self-need for a selfobject gift. Addicts
who experience the substance they use and its effects
as an aid to calming and soothing are clearly demonstra-

ting and gratifying archaic self-needs, as are homosexuals who feel mirrored in frantically sought-out episodes of fellatio. Patients who suffer with narcissistic personality disorders do not undergo protracted fragmentation states; their fragmentation is transitory, and ordinarily these patients seek relief, complaining of their feelings of isolation and their inability to form and maintain human relationships.

In sum, patients with these self disorders have had failures in their self/selfobject relationships early in life. In effect, they have fixation of their self-developments and thus continue—albeit unconsciously—to effect repeated archaic self/selfobject bonds, but to no avail, since they will shortly reject these relationships.

In the aging patient, one sees the continuation of older patterns of adjustment and adaptation. Thus the continuation into the aging phase of a narcissistic personality disorder is commonplace. It is important for the therapist to make a careful diagnosis so as not incorrectly to label the patient's ongoing or continuing self state as a new reaction to a current fragmentation.

Protracted Fragmentation States

Patients with borderline disorders and psychoses of all kinds demonstrate not only a heightened vulnerability to self-fragmentation, but also a protracted quality to their fragmentation. When a borderline patient develops a fragmentation state that is followed by a reality-testing loss (psychosis), derailing, and other symptoms of an acute psychotic decompensation, these pathological states may persist for a long time. Further, these patients do not have an adequate capacity to form a therapeutic self/selfobject dyad based on an alliance of effort to appreciate their inner mental lives. These patients commonly experience an absence of as-if transference phenomena and develop a transference psychosis, insisting that the therapist feels this or that and now wishes to cause the patient harm. Thus, in all such patients who have protracted fragmentations, the history reveals that the patient was and is the victim of grossly inadequate selfobject dyads. The result of these failures was the absence of internalization of selfobject functioning (such as admiring), and thus the selves of these people are permanently liable to fragmentation.

In the syndromes we are about to describe, the aging phase of life, with its particular stresses, has evoked intrapsychic tension and breakdown in the elderly self sufficient to cause symptoms of neuroses or of the personality disorders.

Episodic fragmentation disorders

Episodic fragmentations or near-fragmentations are self states in which the self is in need of merging with a revered leader or a mirroring selfobject, albeit temporarily, to overcome a trauma great enough to cause a fragmentation of the self. The self-need that has provoked the seeking of such an encounter is a loss of esteem or a threatened loss of worth in an interpersonal encounter or interenvironmental encounter in which the elderly self suddenly experiences a failure, a loss, or an impending withdrawal of an important person. The withdrawal or threatened withdrawal of the significant source of worth or the fear of one's own separa-

tion through illness or death evokes the fragmentation—total or partial, chronic or episodic—that requires
repair. In the instance of the episodic fragmentation,
implying a shortened time frame and a lack of intensity,
the repair ordinarily will be of the mature selfobject encounter in which friends or trusted caretakers, recognizing the flagging self-worth or anxiety, respond with an
infusion of self-worth mirroring and allow themselves
to become a target for idealization, thereby effecting
self-repair.

*Self fragmentation resulting in neurotic syndromes in the
elderly*

A neurotic syndrome is one of the possible outcomes
of a self in fragmentation. In a fragmented self, the
drives are now in a free state, not bound with the assertiveness of a cohesive self and not contained, if possible,
by the defenses of the psyche. In the elderly, such an
outpouring of *drive* can result in defenses of projection
or of projection, displacement, and ultimately avoidance (the elements of a phobia), and with these defenses, the primary gain—the reduction of anxiety that
constitutes the success of the neuroses. The *fragmentation* in the elderly self after the death of a spouse or
caretaker sometimes is resolved when the person affected becomes permanently frightened and unable to
leave the house, fearing catastrophe if he or she goes
into the outside world, an agoraphobia.

In other instances, where the fragmentation has resulted in a neurotic syndrome in which emerging drives
during a fragmentation have elicited new (to the individual) or intensified defenses, the drives of sadism or

lust may not be immediately visible or may never be visible to others. The observer sees only the mechanisms of projection, displacement, isolation, undoing or repression and conversion. Similarly, the observer cannot witness the conflict between the drive and the conscience, the dialectic that renders the naked drive unacceptable to discharge and forces defensive action on the part of the self.

At times, the *drives* evoked and the *fears* and *defenses* evoked in an *elderly self* in a *fragmented condition* resemble a "return of the neurosis of the past" in which an elderly self reacting to a major stress reexperiences the neurosis of childhood. Such was the case (Chapter 5) when a patient, after a major stress (a life-threatening illness), reexperienced her fears of and preoccupations with dirt and being dirty and redeveloped old hand washing and cleaning rituals. In this case of the return of a compulsive-obsessive neurosis, the patient, after a major stress (the fear of death and with it the threatened loss of her selfobject world), reexperienced the complete neurosis of her childhood—the drives and its defenses, and with them the primary gain of the repression of her *anxious* thoughts about her dissolution.

In summary, the neurotic syndromes—whether phobic states, compulsive-obsessive neurosis, or hysterias—are one of the possible outcomes of an elderly self in fragmentation. The observer cannot always "see" the so-called drives in conflict, but is witness to complaints of a "destructive elevator" or a "destructive physician" or to a hand-washing ritual or to expressions of shameful, hostile thoughts. One is inclined to describe these syndromes in the elderly as neurotic-*like* syndromes since data on the emerging drives in conflict so often are missing or cannot be obtained.

The narcissistic personality and behavior disorders in the elderly

As previously described, the narcissistic personality in early life represents a failure of functioning of the selfobject caretakers, resulting in an *enfeebled* self searching for self-enrichment, with an archaic selfobject, but never able fully to unfold to anyone for fear of rebuff. Other painful symptoms include the waves of low esteem (the empty depression) and hypochondriasis and the inability to calm oneself.

In the elderly self, a syndrome is revealed that resembles the narcissistic personality disorder emanating from the emotional climate in which the major sources of exogenous narcissistic supplies—affirmation, calming, and soothing—become deficient or absent. Of course, these syndromes are prominent in those whose *need* for external reminders of their worth is a major factor in maintaining their equilibrium. Such is the case with persons whose self-sustenance is maintained in no small measure by their spouses, the "death-of-love" syndrome in the elderly self. These syndromes are also prominent in those selves in which, directly after retiring or decreasing of their activities, they discover to their dismay that with the rewards of becoming the monarch emeritus or parent emeritus, the mirroring of their selves shrinks. And with the "death of love" or the shrinking of selfobject rewards alleviated by compensatory gratifications comes the presentation of the narcissistic deficiency syndrome in the elderly self.

Among the painful symptoms are the feelings of aloneness and emptiness, the hypersensitivity to insult or lack of "appropriate" recognition, the waves of inferiority (without guilt, the empty depression), the agitation, and the walling-off behavior, mixed with attempts at securing contact with selfobjects. Vulnerability to fragmentation is an important feature of these narcissistic deficiency syndromes.

Common Stressors in the Elderly that Induce Psychopathology

In each developmental phase, there are environmental situations that are experienced as stressful, and so it is in the elderly phase of life. The situations that cause psychic pain in the elderly include the loss of significant objects and selfobjects; illnesses both of themselves and of others of importance to them; interpersonal difficulties; and a host of situations in the culture, including economic hardship.

The Losses

To many elderly people, the losses of people who were important to them are the most difficult hardships to bear. Those losses that involve persons who were sources of narcissistic supplies (selfobjects, archaic and mature) are especially significant as they can precipitate an episodic fragmentation or a more protracted fragmentation and the advent of the narcissistic personality disorder. Such a situation might be that of the death of a spouse who had functioned for the remaining spouse as a selfobject in many instances. The resulting self/selfobject rupture, without a compensatory source of selfobject supplies, in turn might result in the empty, lonely, depressed narcissistic deficiency state of the narcissistic personality disorder (the death of love).

Another major loss for the elderly is that of vitality and leadership and the mastery of one's surroundings. In those to whom receptive strivings have been permanently unacceptable, the loss of control is a major stress, leading to fearful dependency and chronic discontent throughout the elderly phase.

Another major stressor for the elderly is the advent of chronic illness, resulting in the entry into forced passivity, pain, and immobilization. Whether the illness is of the elderly person or of the person's caretaker, it marks the end of active life, and with it, the inability to gain emotional rewards—mirroring, soothing—from one's own activities, and thus represents a major loss of narcissistic supplies. Such is also the case when there is significant *deterioration* through arthropathy or memory deficiencies or deterioration of the posterior columns of the spinal chord. Once again, the person is deprived of activities—piano playing, writing, computer programming, performing surgery—that were major methods of deriving emotional nurturance, and therefore the loss of these abilities is especially tragic.

Another major stressor in the elderly leading to a diminution of their ordinary sources of narcissism and self-balance is their altered relationships with their caretakers. In some cultures and families, they are reacted to with phobic *avoidance*, with their relatives shunning them because they are weak and are close to the all-frightening phenomena of death. In other instances, the transformation from being a dependent of the aged relative to being a caretaker is never made, and thus relatives of the now-needy elderly person never become caretakers of the person's welfare. The transition from self/selfobject to selfobject/self has not been made.

The Culture and Its Economics

Yet another drain on the well-being of the elderly is the economic situation in which they often find themselves. The status of pension and Social Security funds reflect the financial well-being of the society, and so the depression–prosperity cycle has a major impact on the well-being of the elderly. In times of inflation, the fixed pension funds suffer, and with this imbalance comes a major fear—that of having to live with a relative or in the dreaded nursing home (Baldwin & Jolley, 1986; Brody, 1985; Jarvik & Small, 1982).

This survey of the stressors on the elderly self reminds the observer that being old in our culture is not for the weak. The effects of the stressors all too often are responsible for the elderly self being at high risk for becoming fragmented. The outcome of such a fragmentation might be the emergence of a neurotic syndrome, a narcissistic personality disorder, or a depression (Gitelson, 1948; Goldfarb, 1955; Rivlin & Wiener, 1988).

The next chapter will offer a model for the diagnosis and psychotherapeutic treatment of the elderly.

4

The Psychotherapies for the Elderly Self: Diagnoses and Plans

In performing psychotherapy for the elderly, it is especially important to have a complete diagnosis of the patient's self-deficits and of the areas of the self that are intact, as well as an awareness of the intactness or deficits in the patient's mentational processes. This is the process of establishing the so-called empathic diagnosis. Another essential task is that of matching the difficulties and strengths of the self of the patient with the appropriate therapy, the therapeutic diagnosis.

THE EMPATHIC DIAGNOSIS AND THE ASSESSMENT OF BRAIN FUNCTIONS

The empathic diagnosis represents a first phase of any psychotherapy in which the therapist gathers the *cognitive* data of the words and affects and other nonverbal behaviors and adds the empathic data to form a picture of the self. In each case, it is hoped, the therapist will be able to have several sessions in which to establish a diagnosis since this is essential to the success of the psychotherapy. Moreover, it is of special importance when treating the elderly to be careful not only in evaluating the details of the behavior, the cognitive observations, but in carrying out the sometimes difficult task of seeing the world through the eyes of the patient, the empathic view. Empathy, the attempt to ferret out memory traces in oneself that approximate the self state of the subject being observed, is difficult with the elderly, and thus reference to literary figures and remembrances of other patients may be necessary in order to initiate the empathic process.

The next stage in our diagnostic workup is to organize the data of cognition and empathy into a model of the mind that will enable us ultimately to prescribe an appropriate therapy for the self we are examining. With regard to the elderly self, we must pose the following queries: What is deficient in this patient's self-functioning in any of the areas of the self—from his or her self-worth to his or her self-values? What is deficient in this patient's mentational processes or other organ systems? What areas of the self are working well?

At the conclusion of our diagnostic workup, we wish to be able to offer a profile of the scrutinized self that asserts that the self we have observed is either basically cohesive with self-observing functions that are intact or is deficient in one or many of the self functions, such as a mirror-hungry or ideal-hungry self or an overall enfeebled self or an empty self. Have we been witness to a self that has collapsed as the result of the loss of an archaic selfobject spouse or to a self that is empty owing to its inability to alter its ideals in the process of becoming an elderly self?

THE THERAPEUTIC DIAGNOSIS

After the work of the empathic diagnosis has been completed, the therapist is able to match the findings of the empathic diagnosis with a particular therapeutic modality. Each therapy has as its end point a particular goal, and each therapy requires certain self-capacities of its candidates. The task of the therapeutic diagnosis is to match the findings of the empathic diagnosis with one of the three major therapeutic modalities or combinations of modalities in terms of goals of outcome for the patient and required capabilities of the patient. These three major psychotherapeutic modalities are supportive psychotherapy, psychoanalytic psychotherapy, and psychoanalysis. As will be discussed in greater detail at a later point, each of these psychotherapies in the elderly may require family consultations, consultations with other health professionals, or the use of pharmacotherapy, either by the therapist, if so qualified, or through referral to a pharmacotherapist.

Supportive Psychotherapy

Supportive psychotherapy is the recommended therapy for those selves that are in disarray—that is, they are in disequilibrium, either depressed or fragmented, and at the time of being observed are unable to join with the therapist to study their intrapsychic distress from the point of view of the genesis of their difficulties or through the institution of dynamic understanding. It is important to state and restate that the restitution of self-equilibrium ordinarily proceeds from the establishment of a self/selfobject bond, the major therapeutic process and goal of supportive psychotherapy. There are instances in which the patient might require, in addition to the selfobject bond, medication for sleep or occasional tranquilizers or antidepressant drugs. The credential required for supportive psychotherapy to proceed is that the patient be able to experience trust in a human encounter so as to form the curative therapeutic bond. Should this capacity not be present (the patient derives little or no comfort from the session), then pharmacotherapy is recommended. In the elderly, an additional criterion is that the patient be able to attend to the material at hand, that is, be sufficiently intact cognitively to comprehend the substance of the interactions (Muslin & Val, 1987).

Psychoanalytic or Sector Psychotherapy

Psychoanalytic or sector psychotherapy is the therapy of choice for those elderly persons who present with a specific psychological problem. They are not currently in disequilibrium and thus have intact self-observing functions. Further, the problem involved is a *specific* problem, and the patients do have intact selves and function well in a variety of ways. The goals of this modality are to alleviate, through insight and the self-enhancing of a basic self/selfobject transference bond, a specific psychological symptom. A clinical example would be a patient who feels unable to leave the house, but who is not fragmented and does not require psychoanalysis. Thus the therapeutic approach of sector psychotherapy involves the therapist and patient working together to study the genesis of the patient's distress by uncovering the patient's inner experiences and background.

Psychoanalysis

The final therapeutic diagnosis is that involving psychoanalysis, a therapy recommended for the self caught up in a pervasive and repetitive state of distress in many areas, but *not* in the gross disequilibrium of fragmentation or depression, thus without operational self-observing functions. These are patients who do have intact self-observing functions, but whose generalized self-distress requires the intensive experience of a focus on the transference onto the therapist for its cure.

DIAGNOSTIC CASE VIGNETTES

Case 1. Mr. E.G.

Mr. E.G., a 76-year-old businessman, sought relief for a loss of interest in life coupled with a painful aloneness. The aloneness, which had been chronic, had intensified over the past few years. He was aware, he stated, that these experiences of futility and aloneness had been emerging since he decided to hand over the reins of the company he had built to his two sons and concentrate on other interests. Over the past six months, he had begun to feel that his family and former colleagues were avoiding him. While he continued to visit his offices daily, in his view, fewer people contacted him, and employees seemed to walk past his office door without even a token salutation for the "old man." His wife and he had then embarked on a series of trips to foreign countries, places he had always wished to visit. However, his mood of despair continued, and even intensified, during his travels, and so he interrupted his holiday and returned home. When his mood of isolation and grief persisted, he consulted his physician, who referred him for consultation.

Mr. E.G.'s initial interviews revealed a well-attired, well-groomed man whose voice was quiet, whose movements were sparse, and whose face was sad. He could not, as he said, attain any relief for his loneliness from his devoted wife, his club, or his possessions—nothing diminished this pervasive experience.

In relating his background, he described a classic rags-to-riches saga. Coming to this country as a teenager, after fighting through many years of poverty and deprivation, he was able to reach the top of his field. An exciting and frightening passage to ultimate achievement, it was one in which he always experienced a sense of purpose and a heightened sense of self-value. Perhaps the most important perquisites of his achievements, the most important accoutrements of power, were the acknowledgments of his status, from the salutations of the doormen to the effusive greetings of his secretaries and staff; these responses were for him the infusion of worth for which he lived. Another important striving was described in his need for minute-to-minute control of his life, so that he would not be in the self state of aloneness. In his heyday, each moment of his daily living had been accounted for, each evening was booked for social or business functions and weekends were planned far in advance. Many minutes of his hectic week were devoted to rounding out his schedule so that he would know where he would be weeks later. Even with all these attempts to avoid "empty time," as he labeled it, he continued to suffer a symptom from childhood: upon arising each morning, he would experience an overwhelming sensation of total painful aloneness that was almost paralyzing in its intensity.

Aloneness in adult life reflects the residue of a self bereft of adequate recognition from empathic selfobjects. In Mr. E.G.'s background in his country of origin, his life indeed had been marked by unresponsiveness on the part of those around him. The youngest of seven children, he had minimal contact with his mother, and little contact with his older siblings. He remembered with great sadness and bitterness that he had constantly begged his mother not to leave him to go to her daily work in her husband's shop. He remembered—or fantasized—being in his crib, wet and hungry and crying, but alone, and unable to elicit any help from his environment. He realized that he had a difficult childhood. He was a bed-wetter, had anorexia, sucked his thumb, suffered from insomnia, and had had great difficulty in reading (which persisted as an adult). Early in life, he had learned to extract recognition from his world by "hustling." He started working as a delivery boy at the local bakery when he was seven years old and soon began to receive praise for his "hustling" ways. He was always able to run faster than anyone else to deliver the goods. He left school before he was 10, by that time having learned to master his world through massive outbursts of energy directed toward the acquisition of goods and the domination of other people. When he was 18, he owned his own business; when he was 25, he was an established figure in the industry that he had entered. Wherever he went, he was in control; all of his business and social interactions centered on him. For many decades, he functioned in this manner designed to sustain his receptive needs but always outside of his self-awareness. He never revealed himself to anyone, and never asked for assistance or guidance—or companionship. He simply became the executive officer, in control of business 18 hours a day and in control of all human interactions.

Here are segments from his initial interviews:

Mr. E.G.: Well, Doc, what can I tell you? It's all a big joke, on me! Bust my ass all these years for what? Everybody's always said I'm the greatest salesman there ever was—look what it got me (quiet for a long time). Maybe if I stayed down south, never came back to see the company again. *(quiet)* I drop in, they all give me the big hello, but I can see their eyes are looking behind me to their office to see how fast they can get away. My sons—wow! They shuttle me in and out so fast I think I'm in the presence of royalty and I'm a *shlepper* asking favors. It sure was different when I gave it to them—parties, plaques. Everybody down there looks at me,

I can see it, with pity. You know, when I go there, I begin to act funny myself, I try to listen in through the doors, I look through their mail—hell, they're not including me in, so what should I do? I got no place in the sun. What should I do?

And then at home. I *never, never*, was good at being at home. Here it is May and I know where I'm going New Year's Eve. I mean I got to be on the move, I got to make sure I'm going somewhere every night. She's always yelling at me, "Can't we stay home? What's wrong with staying home?" I'll tell you because I can't tell her. She's a nice lady but she don't talk much. She starts to talk to someone, then she looks at me—for 50 years—and she says, "Tell him what I mean." Being with her is boring, but the last year has been worst. We put on the early news at night and I look over and she's sleeping—all the time. Then I get more restless and I go to the phone and I start callin' and callin' and callin'. I finally get someone to talk to, at least for awhile. So I don't take chances like that. I make sure we're doin' something. (*gets up and paces for a while*).

I already told you that morning stuff. I get up—always, since I was a kid—and oh man, it's so lonely. She's right next to me but it's like lookin' at a dead person when I look at her sleepin'. It ain't easy to get up, I just stay there like I'm stuck. I can't get up. I could, maybe I should, get up and get out of there. Maybe I should wake her up, I don't know. It's such an awful feelin'. I get almost a little nuts. I get shaky and stuck. It's so dark, wow!

So what can you do for me? What should I do? My guy told me you can help me. Can you? I'm pretty far gone. Course it don't mean much. I mean I'm old already.

At a later point, he said of his background:

What was it like? Well we were O.K. as far as essentials. We always had something on the table, nothing fancy.

They were hard working. Well, she was, for sure. He just couldn't do it without her. His store was, you know, dry goods. She just got up every day, made somethin', and went down. I just remember being alone a lot, nobody with me. Everybody for himself. It was lonely. Nobody was, you might say, for me, even though I was little (*quiet for a long time*).

Did I tell you how long it took me to read? I never read now to pass the time. No one really watched me. When I stopped going to school, no one really knew. I just kept workin' one week in a row and no one noticed.

At a later point in the interviews, he said:

We got to Ellis Island when I was 13. It was my brother Sam and my two next sisters then. The rest stayed back till later. All of a sudden, my mother and the two girls were taken to another place and my father and me and my brother had to stay on those benches—for eight days. They brought us graham crackers and milk. I never had graham crackers before. It was lonely. I was very sad, no one talked to us, we didn't talk to each other. I was a little kid and it was a long time ago but you know, I never thought I'd see my ma any more. (*quiet for two minutes*). So now you know me. Can you do anything for me?

The empathic diagnosis

This diagnosis represents a description of the self state of the patient. What is amiss and what is functioning adequately or well? In the elderly, it is necessary carefully to appraise the organic functions of memory and comprehension and difficulties in orientation—episodic or pervasive. A special aspect of the diagnostic workup of the elderly is to learn of the physical difficulties of the patient *and* any medications being taken, such as for hypertension or irritable bowel syndrome, that might be affecting the patient's emotional state. If the therapist is not familiar with the effects of the various compounds on the psyche, a consultation should be arranged with the medical practitioner.

In the case of Mr. E.G., the empathic diagnosis was that he was experiencing a collapse of his self, at times approaching a frank disarray. From the data available at the time of the diagnostic interviews, his life had been consumed in no small part by carrying out what might be called the actions of "compensatory grandiosity," actions designed to eke out whatever morsels of mirroring would be available to him. These activities were attempts at repair of the self-deficits incurred from an absent set of archaic selfobjects and with no surrogate selfobjects to infuse him either with approval or with leading, calming, and soothing. His was a truly self-made self. As he stated, "I was always on the make." His remarkably successful life was a tribute to his courage, although, as was described, the symptoms of narcissistic deficit had always hounded him—the loneliness, the inability to calm himself, the basic aloofness manifested by his need *always* to be in control of his life and never to be overtly dependent on anyone. Other manifestations of his narcissistic state emerged later; for example, the compulsive sexuality that did offer him mirroring and the ephemeral calming after sexual union.

The therapeutic diagnosis

From the empathic diagnosis emerges the prescription for the appropriate provisional therapy. Each therapy is on probation so to speak; further evaluation will determine the correctness of the therapy. In the case of Mr. E.G., the immediate prescription was for the balm of a self/selfobject bond, which, it was hoped, would do the job of calming his troubled self and also be of service in direction giving to ease the pain of his, at that time, directionless self. This is the required task of supportive therapy—the institution of a selfobject bond to provide the missing functions of the patient's self-in-disarray. Mr. E.G.'s deficits were derived from a background absent of selfobject supports. For so many years he had been striving to procure recognition through his hyperactive business and social life. His need for calming and soothing was also a prominent deficit in this, the retirement phase of his life. At the point at which he entered therapy, his self-observing functions were not sufficiently intact to allow us to uncover with him the underlying difficulties in his life that led to the self-collapse. His lifelong practice of defending himself against bonding with people to maintain his cohesiveness could *not* be a focus of therapeutic activity at this point.

Case 2. Mr. S.T.

At his initial diagnostic interviews, the patient was noted to be a tall, gray-haired man, well-groomed and attired in a well-fitting business suit. He smiled cordially and shook hands with enthusiasm. However, his gait was slow, and as soon as he sat down, his shoulders slumped and his face caved in.

Mr. S.T.: Doctor, I've come to see you because my internist believes I need *your* kind of help. He had me on two kinds of pills, one at night, one during the day. But as you can see from my smiling face (*smiles and then sighs*), I'm not much better. (*long pause*) I guess I'm depressed. I certainly am not happy. I don't know, here I am at 72 without direction. My wife doesn't know what to do. I've never really included her in my career anyway. Frankly, I don't believe I can make a decision—isn't that the height of stupidity? (*quiet for one minute*) Here's what it's all about in my amateur way of thinking about it. *I* thought it was time for me to retire. I heard such good things about it from my lawyer friends. You know, the travel, the life of leisure with golf and games and no responsibilities. So I told my partners that when I am 74, that'll be it. No one seemed to object at the firm. I'm ashamed to say that I do *not* look forward to a life of trips. (*stops talking, the face collapses, and his eyes fill with tears*) But, you know, my wife started bustling around, started talking about Florida and cruises. I don't want to disappoint her. I don't want to disappoint the guys at work, now they're all expecting the old man to go. (*quiet for one minute*) Life is certainly always filled with surprises, not a whole lot of them pleasant. I've forgotten now what my great motivation was in wanting to retire. Did *I* really believe a life of slowdown was going to satisfy me and the wife? Maybe I truly believed at that time that I had worked hard enough and that I would enjoy the trips and reading more and not being a slave to the the alarm clock and the deadlines for the contracts to be filed. I think I did. I don't know what I think now, I'm so down in the dumps. Most of the time—it's so stupid—I do not give a damn. I'm just going to work in a leaden fashion. You know, I'm just a big bag of heavy nothing. After all these years of lawyering, I have nothing. I have nothing because I lost my interest. I really don't care about anything. Without interest, I'm a cadaver. I suppose that's where it's all at. (*silence*) You know, at this moment I can't remember *anything* I've ever done. (silence) And then I get confused—my mouth feels like it's filled with ashes. Probably because my insides are not working and I don't eat or drink unless someone reminds me. And all day long, I'm pulling my body along because it's like it's inert. I feel every ache and pain in all my muscles. A total stupid mess. (*silence; eyes fill with tears*) That too! I have these bursts of emotionality, but over what?

Mr. S.T. was clearly in a depression, showing all the classical mental signs and symptoms and the so-called vegetative signs—the malaise, appetite loss, gastrointestinal changes. He also was able to reveal a major precipitant to the self-collapse he was experiencing, the retirement from his profession of over three decades. He was aware that the self-changes he was suffering were stimulated by his coming retirement, but he was unaware of what became mobilized in his self that eventuated in the depression. He was not aware of what would be lost to him if he were to remove himself from his profession; he was not aware of the psychological role that his profession had played in his self economy, the narcissistic (self-love) balance. For Mr. S.T., his profession had served as a external source of worth that was as vital to him as is applause from a mirroring self-object in one's infancy. What he was aware of at the time of his interview was only that he suddenly felt that life was without importance; his ability to value his wants and his interests was now so diminished that any project, such as retirement, was of no consequence to him. He was experiencing a narcissistic (self-love or self-worth or self-regard) deficit, a reaction to the impending loss of what had become—we infer—a major source of narcissistic supplies, his role as an attorney. That Mr. S.T. was in dire need of supplies from the "outside," so to speak, assumes that his endogenous sources of worth were not sufficient to maintain a cohesive self.

All the preceding remarks point to an empathic diagnosis of an enfeebled self, a self in disequilibrium, in crisis, as a result of massive loss—real or imagined—of a source of worth. This crisis, this self in disequilibrium, required the help of supportive therapy, the specific therapy of a crisis condition aimed at effecting a self/ selfobject bond. In Mr. S.T.'s situation, albeit he would later need to *understand* his reactions to his plans for retirement, at the time he presented for therapy, he required the balm of a self/selfobject bond.

The specific selfobject functions that were required at the time of his initial interviews were the functions of leadership—the calm and firm direction required by the floundering self in need of a powerful guide who knows the way to intrapsychic peace. In Mr. S.T.'s situation, it was clear that he could not, at the time of his interviews, retire from his profession. And so the diagnostic interviews became therapeutic interviews, since the therapeutic diagnosis was that he required immediate supportive psychotherapy.

The following is a segment from a subsequent interview.

Mr. S.T.: I didn't go to the office today because I simply couldn't go down there in my condition. I didn't do anything at home, just looked at some books, listened to some music, walked around a little bit.
Therapist: Now that we've heard the difficulties you've

been having since declaring your retirement, it certainly sounds like your retirement plans have thrown you into a depression.

Mr. S.T.: Do you really believe that?

Therapist: Well, we've got a lot to understand about you to pin down what got stirred up in you after you decided to retire, but it seems clear that your plans for retirement have had quite a negative effect on you. It turns out that many people cannot retire, that their work is a major source of worth; without work, it is very hard to survive for many of us.

Mr. S.T.: You know, I've been working since I was a kid, before I was a teenager. Back then, it was needed to survive. But yeah, I've been at it all my life. Vacations and I never have been a good match. Yeah, working has been my whole life. Since I was 6 or 7 years old, delivering newspapers, and then—oh so many other jobs. Hell, even during law school, I held jobs. (*brightens up*) I guess I've been a workaholic all my days. (*quiet, sad*) Well, what are you saying, Doctor, that I cannot retire? That I should not retire? What are you suggesting? There's a lot of people involved here. I told my partners, my wife, my friends. What kind of fool am I to go forth and back and back and forth?

The patient floundered again at this point, but communicated by the burst of anxiety— "What are you saying?"—that he needed the selfobject functions of the leader who assumes command. What this patient required was for the therapist acting-as-the-selfobject to take over. Although not enough was known of this patient to give a final therapeutic diagnosis, it was sufficient that this therapeutic strategy could be used.

Therapist: At this moment, I believe it is important to call a halt to your plans for retirement. It will give us a chance to calm everything down and help you get back in equilibrium. It may be that at a later date you'll want to think of retirement, but at this moment, you're not psychologically ready. In fact, it's made you ill.

Mr. S.T.: What do I tell my people? My wife will kill me.

Therapist: I believe what you tell your people is very important. Telling people that you've put your plans for retirement on the back burner or that you've not ready to retire or are not in a retirement mood yet—all these ways of explaining your reluctance to quit work are easy to understand for those who know you.

Mr. S.T.: Well that's true. (*brightens again*) There were a lot of surprised faces when I announced retirement. My wife though, that's going to be a difficult one, I'll tell you. I don't know, she's made a lot of plans. I don't know. She's not easy to live with when she's disappointed. I'll have to think about it. You're pretty sure I'm not ready to retire, is that it?

Several sessions of a similar nature followed, each time with the therapist advising against retirement, each time with the patient becoming enthusiastic about giving up his retirement plans. However, each time he reminded himself of his wife's needs, he retreated from the idea of not retiring.

During the ninth diagnostic/therapeutic session, he said:

> I guess I always knew that I had to work, to achieve, in order for me to be in good shape. Hell, Sunday was always the worst day of the week. It goes back a long way in my house, I guess I always got my cup of tea for being a good kid, a hardworking kid. My mother had her hands full. We were poor; times were bad when I was growing up. My sister was not well. She was older, but I was the one who brought in money, not her. She kept my mother and father crazy with her idiosyncracies and her tantrums. But not me, hell, I always got the medals for good behavior, good grades.
>
> I tell you, Doctor, I'm coming around to your idea that I should scuttle my idea—at least temporarily—to retire. And I must tell, whether it's meeting with you or the idea of not retiring, I'm feeling better. I got up today and I attacked my breakfast. I'm still blue from time to time. I also have to tell you that I lied to my wife, I couldn't tell her flat out. I told her the firm's billing this year was too low, that they needed what I brought in, and that I couldn't leave in the near future. Oh, she didn't like that, I can tell you, but she bought it, at least for now. I know you think that's chicken on my part, but it's easier than to get into it with her. She can never understand me. I've never told her my troubles; she attacks me when I do. I always have

to present an untroubled front to her. She gets dis-
combobulated when she sees me sick or tired or
nervous. It's not worth it.

Now that the patient's acute distress was waning after
a dozen interviews, the therapeutic diagnosis for his
future psychotherapy had to be made. The problem presented to the psychotherapist was that his present self
state was resistant to the changes necessary to enter
into the aging phase of his life. Moreover, his marriage
supported his resistance to physiological slowdown and
to the unfolding of his needs for nurturance and leadership. On the surface, the marriage appeared to be a
repetition of his previous life, with his mother/sister
exacting control over him to provide for them.

After a few more sessions in which the patient continued to improve in his mood and vigor, the therapist
informed him that it would be advisable for him to continue in therapy, twice a week, to help him understand
the factors that ushered in his depression, that is, to
enter into intensive psychotherapy.

In terms of the patient's credentials for intensive psychotherapy, he revealed the capacity to form a bond to
achieve equilibrium and to ally himself with the therapist to study himself.

In terms of the therapeutic need to enter into this form
of therapy, the patient's problem was limited enough to
be a focus of the work of intensive psychotherapy—the
fear of dependency, especially as acted out with his wife
and his work life. The therapeutic diagnosis of intensive
psychotherapy is reserved for those conditions in which
a specific psychological problem that can be illuminated

is present. Patients selected for intensive psychotherapy cannot be in a self-crisis since the requirement for such patients is that they have intact self-observing functions, that is, that they can ally themselves with their therapists to observe their experiences. In a self-crisis of intense depression or anxiety, the patient's functions of self-observing are ordinarily not working nor does the patient have the capacity for studying his or her experiences with a therapeutic ally. These patients are too caught up in their strivings for calming or approval.

Mr. S.T.'s difficulties in life were not widespread at this point; he had been able to derive gratification in many areas of work and play. Those patients who have widespread self difficulties and are not in a crisis of depression or anxiety should be thought of as candidates for psychoanalysis if they have the credentials to pursue this form of psychotherapy.

In sum, Mr. S.T.'s specific problem was that of a lifelong reliving of an old way to carry on: contain all outbreaks of needs for direction and nurturance and be of service—accommodate, adjust—in each relationship and in each endeavor. Once he could achieve the status of the compleat accommodator, he would experience a sense of well-being, since, in his psyche, being of service was equated with obtaining the requisite mirroring. Work allowed him to experience worth; conversely, dependency was equated with rejection and, therefore, aloneness.

The lifelong experience of unconsciously maintaining the controls over his needs was clearly demonstrated in two instances that represented *the* self problem for which he required intensive psychotherapy: his relationship with his wife and his relationship with his profession. In both situations, the patient had been living the archaic way—containing his needs, advancing his capacities to be the accommodator, becoming anxious if his defenses of being the pleaser were to fail, as would be the case if his needs became intense.

Case 3. Ms. C.H.

The following discussion focuses on the empathic and therapeutic diagnoses of patients who require psychoanalysis as their psychotherapeutic method of obtaining psychic relief. In the case of Ms. C.H., she entered her therapy with the initial complaints that she had become "bitter and blue" over the past several years. Her next associations dealt with her reactions to the death of her spouse. At the time of these initial interviews, Ms. C.H. was a sad figure, dressed in black and moving slowly. These sessions dealt with an attempt on the therapist's part to ease the pain of isolation Ms. C.H. was experiencing by effecting a therapeutic bond. After some weeks, the isolation was diminished and she began telling of lifelong attitudes of bitterness and futility and a history of failed or disappointing relationships, including the relationship she had had with her late husband.

The following is a segment of one of the sessions in which it became clear that she was a candidate for psychoanalysis.

Ms. C.H.: Yes, I am feeling somewhat better, less heavy as I walk, although I can't concentrate on my writing nor can I read deeply. Oh well, nothing much is lost to the world if I can't write again. (*quiet, silent*) I've yet to hear from my sisters and I've called them several times. Just another one of those who've been a disappointment to me. I'm always initially eager to set up some contact with some person—so often a woman—and then something happens and it's over. I don't know, maybe it's me. I've started and quit so many things. What am I looking for? Nothing has satisfied me for years. That's funny (*no laughter or display of mirth*) since I've *never* been satisfied with anyone or anything ever. You know it's true (*tearful voice*), I've never been satisfied. For some reason or other, maybe discussing with you, I've been thinking, and even dreaming—an old lady, can you imagine?—about my background, my crazy mother, my crazy father, my crazy sisters. Oh, what's the difference? Who can help this? No one, right?

Therapist: You haven't given up hope that you *can* be in a better state of mind than you've been. Our sessions so far have evoked in you that hope, that optimism.

Ms. C.H.: Yes, but that has been my signature. I do get involved, but then I get disappointed or I just turn away or I feel trapped and I sabotage. It's all mixed up, my love affair with the world. (*quiet*) The point is (*quiet for one minute*) that no one, I mean *no one* can unravel the mystery. Oh, the other craziness is that I find myself following people around—my cleaning woman for God's sake! I sometimes listen to her. All of a sudden, I'll ask her something and listen, I mean really listen. Now isn't that stupid!

Right now, I'm not feeling bad here. But I can get alone and down in a hurry. I don't mean now. I guess it was always that way.

I think my mother may have been the stupidest ninny in the 20th century. She just knew nothing about anything, except to make such a fetish about how my sisters and I looked. It was all looks and what was acceptable in the society in which we lived. That's all she lived for, to get us ready for marriage to look up to that fool. The answer to every question I had was always, "Wait until your dad comes home." What a ninny.

And there was Dad. Such a funny little man. An owlish face, a perpetual silly look on his face, but he was nice and he was at least somewhat interested in my writing as a youngster. It's too late, much too late to sort out all this craziness and what's happened to me, I know. I can just tell you, I've never—isn't that astonishing?—never got altogether caught up in anyone or anything. In my marriage, I really don't know what made me get so upset after he became sick. I was never caught up with him either. I guess I felt sorry for him. Maybe I felt no one was *ever* going to be there to be a presence for me. So what do you think?

What I thought was that this patient had unfolded a tragic history of deprivation, a self-disturbance of maintaining barriers against deep contact with people and ideas and things. Moreover, this constellation of fears, sensitivities, and resistances was a self-pattern, a character or personality disorder.

The empathic diagnosis of a pervasively enfeebled self, a narcissistic deficit disorder, leads to the therapeutic diagnosis of advising psychoanalysis. Psychoanalysis is the treatment of choice for the empathic diagnosis of a self or character disorder. The therapeutic diagnosis is made when a patient's pervasive difficulties require the intense work of illuminating the heretofore buried self/selfobject longings and conflicts over these longings in a revived interaction with the psychoanalyst—the transference—that will reveal these needs and the fear of and resistance to them. The requirements of the analysands, the patients, are that they are to have, apart from the need and the motivation, a capacity for self-observation and for forming a therapeutic alliance.

In the elderly, rendering the therapeutic diagnosis of psychoanalysis is an even more serious matter than in other age groups, since psychoanalysis requires several visits per week for sustained periods. Therefore, the patient's physical condition—central nervous system, heart, and lungs—must be sound and able to withstand the stress of the psychoanalysis. The analyst must weigh the need for a self-transformation against the effect on the patient's overall physical state. Psychoanalysis is a major undertaking of any age level, but especially so in the elderly since apart from all other considerations mentioned, the analyst must weight the need for the transformed self—the goal of an analysis—against the patient's life span and be prepared to defend the position that the self-changes aimed for in an analysis are sufficiently important to undertake the long and costly project of psychoanalysis.

The next three chapters will consist of detailed descriptions and case histories of the three forms of psychotherapy and combinations of the therapeutic modalities when they are required in the elderly (Muslin, 1974; Muslin & Val, 1987).

5

The Supportive Psychotherapies

In those patients who are experiencing psychic disarray—whether as a result of immobilizing depression or of massive anxiety with self-fragmentation—the therapeutic diagnosis of supportive therapy is made, which implies that the development of the self/selfobject tie or transference between patient and therapist is needed to repair the disequilibrium of the self. For the patient to enter into the curative therapeutic bond, there must be sufficient trust in human encounters—the capacity to feel safe in revealing to another the dilemmas and distresses that have evoked the intrapsychic disarray. Another credential for the candidate for supportive psychotherapy is the ability to transfer onto the therapist selfobject features derived from the patient's selfobject background that are necessary to restore the self-in-disarray.

There are two major obstacles to the therapeutic bond in those patients who cannot form the requisite self/selfobject tie or have difficulties with this task: the *defense against the transference* and the *defense transference*. The defense against the transference in a particular self reflects the residual experience of danger of rejection in the human encounter in those whose infancy and childhood were marked by frequent and protracted rejection by caretakers. The defense transference is the process by which the patient unconsciously transfers onto the therapist those hostile and disappointing features of the major parent in their early lives. At the same time, the patient revives the experiences and executes the behaviors of the archaic defenses against the malevolence, now experienced as emanating from the therapist. Thus this patient will resist or fight back or be obsequious with the therapist-as-parent (Daniels, 1976; Schlessinger & Robbins, 1983), reenacting the ancient methods of keeping the malevolent parent at bay.

There are credentials that a therapist must possess in order to work with the elderly as a supportive psychotherapist. Functioning as a selfobject in any therapeutic encounter with any patient group is experienced by some therapists as deviating from the generally accepted model of the therapist in the psychoanalytic and psychotherapeutic arenas as a blank screen onto which the patient projects his or her unconscious complexes. Therapists, of course, differ widely in their self-makeup and so differ widely in their abilities to "be" a selfobject figure, that is, to function as a mirroring caretaker or selfobject leader in supportive therapy. Other factors, such as the therapist's fatigue, intrapsychic cohesiveness, and transference onto the patient (the therapist's own need to derive comfort from the patient), are all impediments to the difficult work of becoming a supportive psychotherapist.

In work with the elderly, the psychotherapist performing supportive psychotherapy is to "be" a selfobject to a patient who commonly is older or even much older. The therapist is in a psychological position similar to that of the children of the elderly patient, who are required to undergo a self-transformation in order to be a selfobject to one who was formerly the selfobject, to become a caretaker to one's former caretaker and without reluctance and animus that so often mar these encounters (Muslin, 1981). The resistance to these self-transformations reveals the continuing wishes in the therapist—as well as in all younger persons—to be able to continue to derive selfobject gratifications from one's caretaker. The term "reverse Oedipus complex," so frequently found in the literature on geriatric psychotherapy, is an example in my view of the resistance in therapists to "hear" their patients defending themselves against their strivings for dependency on younger therapists by attempting to make daughters and sons of their therapists and in this way attempt to diminish their dependency on them (Zinberg, 1964; Grotjahn, 1955).

The therapist's wish to derive gratifications from the elderly patient may not be immediately evident; at times it appears in the therapist's resistance to terminating a session or to terminating the treatment when that is indicated, which is clearly a wish for the patient to continue in his or her ministrations to the therapist. The wish to please is unconsciously translated into avoiding therapeutic actions that the patient will find unpalatable and so a confrontation or the prescription of a medication might be avoided to guard against displeasing the patient (Muslin & Clarke, 1988).

At times, the therapist's unconscious anger at the pa-

tient's neediness is revealed by an "inability" to function as the needed leader or calmer or admirer. Or the
therapist will not "notice" the patient's depression or
mental deterioration or forget to order a certain
drug—all these behaviors perhaps reflecting the therapist's unconscious inhibitions against leadership, often
coupled with wishes for the patient to take over.

THE COURSE OF SUPPORTIVE PSYCHOTHERAPY
IN THE ELDERLY

Supportive psychotherapy in the elderly commonly falls
into a modal course that goes through four phases: (1)
the establishment of rapport; (2) the defense transference and its neutralization, when present; (3) the formation of the self/selfobject bond and the selfobject activities of the therapist; and (4) the termination.

The Establishment of Rapport

The therapist's first obligation to the patient is to provide an ambience of safety, a haven, for patients to
unfold their problems. For the elderly, this climate of
safety, equanimity, and respect is especially important.
Perhaps the best advice is to regard each elderly patient
as harboring a narcissistically depleted self that requires
constant attention on the therapist's part to the ordinary
details of an interview, such as the proper greeting, the
arrangement of chairs, and the unruffled pleasant and
unobtrusive manner of the careful interviewer. Another
area of responsiveness that assists in the establishment

of rapport is the therapist's awareness of the central nervous system's limitations on verbal and nonverbal behaviors.

The Defense Transference

The cautiousness and inhibitions of the elderly patient at the beginning of the therapy are a mixture of uneasiness and shame at unveiling psychic distress with an as-yet-unknown admixture of defense transference. The therapist has to be prepared for a variable period of "testing the waters" on the part of the patient, which will differentiate the shame/inhibition from the defense transference against the formation of the selfobject bond. At times, the continuance of the defense transference mandates that the therapist interpret this resistance to diminish its hold on the patient.

The Formation of the Self/Selfobject Bond and Selfobject Activities

The communication of the selfobject needs to the therapist is ordinarily accomplished through verbal behaviors that indicate the disarray, although patients may exhibit their selfobject needs through a mixture of verbal and nonverbal behaviors inside and outside the office, thus demonstrating their need for control or soothing. Once the empathic diagnosis of the required selfobject posture is made, the therapist begins the supportive work of being a mirroring selfobject or an idealized parent selfobject.

The Termination

The work of supportive therapy is ended when the symptoms of psychic disequilibrium are reduced or have disappeared. In the elderly, the therapeutic bond is often continued in biweekly, bimonthly, or p.r.n. (as-needed) contacts. These contacts may not be full-fledged interviews, but instead phone calls, letters, and occasional visits, and may be initiated by either the therapist or the patient.

One other aspect of the termination consists in the finding that the elderly patient, while no longer in frank disarray, continues to have circumscribed anxiety or shame and requires referral for intensive psychotherapy.

CASE 1. MR. E.G.*

Mr. E.G., a 76-year-old man, was referred for relief of the depressive symptoms that began to overwhelm him six months after he had retired from the business he founded, which he then passed on to his sons. According to his description of his mental state, he no longer had any interest in life since retirement—neither travel, his marriage, nor friends, nothing, in fact, gave him pleasure. He felt increasing agitation and helplessness and was hopeless concerning the future. In his initial case history, he described a lifelong struggle to gain affirmation for his hungry self. Since his early days in his large family of origin, he had been a "hustler,"

---

*See Chapter 4, pages 59–67, for initial data gathering.

and he continued in this manner until his retirement. He related that he found it necessary to control all aspects of his life, from the time he awoke until he went to sleep at night. He structured his social life so that his calendar was filled 12 months in advance. While seemingly a hail-fellow/well-met type of person, he remained aloof in his personal contacts. He never allowed himself to depend on anyone, except in a limited manner in which he always maintained control over the intensity of the bond. In the early diagnostic interviews, he described the emptiness of his early life—a mother who ran from him to her daily chores at the family business, an unavailable father, and no surrogate selfobjects to fill the void his parents created.

The Course of the Psychotherapy

Phases 1 & 2. The Establishment of Rapport and the Defense Transference

The therapeutic goal for Mr. E.G. was clear: his self was painfully enfeebled and deficient in self-regard and so he needed an infusion of the selfobject charge of mirroring. However, in view of his special history of disappointment and subsequent defensiveness against unfolding himself to objects and selfobjects, the initial phase of therapy was an important one; it was necessary to proceed at his pace and to be very flexible about times, frequency of visits, responses to his queries, and so on. He would make an appointment only after considering five or six alternative times, and then call back to repeat the process. Even though he knew that it was up to the therapist to inform him as to when he would be available, after six or seven months of therapy, he would still call and say, "What about Saturday at 9 a.m.?" The therapist was also asked to tell his wife and some of his children about the diagnosis and give them an overview of the treatment that was required.

After approximately four months, the patient entered into a limited therapeutic bond; he began allowing himself to seek advice and resistance to the therapy diminished—he came to sessions early and stayed until the end and "took in" the therapist and the therapeutic message. Here is a segment from an interview at this stage.

Mr. E.G.: It's hard to get here. I've been driving and driving. Can't you see me earlier? I've been waiting in your waiting room like forever. So what should I talk about today? I worry about what I should talk about every time, don't I? After a while, it goes away. You're not bored? You have to listen to all these complaints all day. Are mine different? I look at you hard all the time. Am I looking to see if you're bored? Well, are you bored? Am I interesting? I'm certainly not an interesting case. An old man without a pot to piss in!

So what are you going to do for me? What you told me the other day I guess was right. I thought about it. What was it exactly? Say it again, that part about my learning to keep people at a safe distance.

But so what? I can't do that forever. Tell me again. Tell me again: What did you say exactly?

Therapist: I said that you had learned early in life to wall yourself off from people so that none could disappoint you again. No one owns you—that's been your motto all your life.

Mr. E.G.: Right. Right. So what do I do now? I'm back to where I was. I don't have a pot to piss in and I'm not about to beg my sons. Goddammit, I own that company—well, I'm still a principal owner, I'm still chairman of the board. It's confused—I can't figure it out for the first time in my life. I can't figure it out. I worked so hard all my life, I don't know how to goof off. I don't know how to quit and look at the four walls.

Therapist: Worked hard and worked well and gave a lot of help to a lot of people.

Mr. E.G.: Work well, so what? (*quiet*) You know, that's true. A lot of people work at that plant. What you said is true, I worked hard, but it's all gone. I don't know what to do. What should I do? I guess I'll just pick her up and go to another place.

Therapist: For so long it's been you alone who made decisions. It's hard to let yourself listen to me and let me into your command room and share the decisions.

Mr. E.G.: Right, yeah, yeah. It's cold here! Don't you have any decent heat?

The capacity of the patient to enter into a bond was limited, but his need to get relief from the loneliness overcame his resistances to the bond, which were clear in this transcribed segment. The therapist offered a defense transference interpretation—once in a general manner and then more specifically related to the resistance against the therapist's ministrations: "It's hard to let yourself listen to me and to let me into your command room and share the decisions." This segment demonstrated the neediness ("Am I interesting?") and the defensiveness ("What can you do for me?").

The behaviors in general were changing and he clearly listened more intently and thought about the sessions afterwards. He also tolerated well a mirroring comment the therapist made for the first time (in the 15th session) that he "had worked hard and well for a long time and was helpful to many people." These comments were true, but it was only at this stage that the therapist felt that Mr. E.G. could accept them without becoming uneasy and, therefore, more resistant.

Phase 3. The formation of the selfobject bond and selfobject activities

The selfobject bond that was called for was actually a mixture: Mr. E.G. had a self depleted of worth and so he required an infusion of mirroring; he also needed calming and direction, and so required the calming and direction of an idealized parent selfobject. The dosing was of importance since his lifelong fear of addiction to people militated against any intense egress of dependency—which would cause a "catastrophic psychological response." And so the selfobject activity had to be carefully titrated against his fear of becoming too merged with the therapist.

The basic selfobject ministrations were two: (1) to attempt to give him a charge of worth, a reminder of his lifelong achievements reflecting his courage as demonstrated in his capacity to tolerate years of hardship to achieve his goals; (2) to direct him to activities in which he could once again gain the applause that was crucial to his self-cohesion.

In supportive psychotherapy, the therapist has to "be" a therapeutic agent since the patient's self at the time of the therapy is incapable of studying the psychic distress and relieving it through uncovering and neutralizing the pathogenic complexes. In this case, Mr. E.G. was relieving his ancient fear of being dependent, which had reemerged as he entered retirement without his lifelong defenses as commander of his destiny against the painfully experienced dependency. Each time he experienced dependency, he reexperienced painful rejection, the abandonment by his people when he became dependent. However, he could not be asked to form an alliance with the therapist to study this fixation as his self was immobilized and no self-observing functions were available to permit him to do so.

The therapist in supportive therapy *acts*; he or she performs selfobject functions as soon as the patient can experience these actions without fear or shame.

Mr. E.G.: I'm sleeping better, but I get those shocks of nerves and I'm very lonely in the morning. I have nowhere to go, do you know that? All these years and nowhere to go. What should I do?

Therapist: I wonder about that. Your advice about the different phases of the business might be advice they could still use. It's only been eight months since you left and you certainly haven't forgotten how to sell, which was your major interest for years. You built a big empire with your selling abilities.

Mr. E.G.: Nah! They don't want me. They don't call. Yes, of course, I built an empire. I could still teach them a thing or two or three. I remember the last time I sold a big order. Oh, what's the use? I gave it up. I'm still chairman of the board. On paper, those boys work for me. (*quiet*)

What are you saying? Hell, I'm not a big-shot consultant. Give advice? What? I don't trust myself. I'm not going to go and suck around my two sons.

Therapist: I'm sure they would be interested in your helping out with some customers whom you developed and serviced through the years. The customers are probably still looking for you when they call.

Mr. E.G.: I'm not going to call and suck around my own sons. I'm too nervous now anyway.

You think I could do it? I'm so lonely—just lonely. I never was lonely at work. What am I going to do with her? She jumps every time I leave the house. How can I leave her now? She got used to me being at home.

You think I could do it?

The patient did begin to visit the plant more regularly and, after a few weeks, asked very cautiously and with much distress in his voice and manner whether he might join his sons on a trip they were planning to visit a major client. The sons agreed with surprise, as they were unaware of the depth of his distress since leaving the company. The selling trip went well and they asked him to come down to the plant more regularly to join in the weekly strategy sessions. He began going to the plant twice a week, and then, after a few months he began visiting the plant for several hours each day.

The patient's mood improved, as did his energy level, and the hopelessness diminished considerably. He seemed to be back into his premorbid self of carving out from his surrounding the emotional nurturance he needed to service his self. He resumed, bit by bit, his high-energy performance of spending his evenings with other people at parties, the theater, dinners, or sporting events. However, the early-morning depression, which had been with him since he was a youngster, continued. In his relationship with the therapist, there now developed a loosening of his standoffish stance, but he continued his posture of being in command. He still tried to "make a deal" over appointment times: a time would be set, he would call and try to change the time, and when unsuccessful, would announce, "I'll have to get back to you." One or two hours later, he would call to state that he would come at the appointed time.

Phase 4. Termination

The patient's initial symptoms were considerably reduced and he was now in equilibrium. He had resumed his work as an important salesperson for his plant, but the administrative duties were permanently delegated to the sons. Thus the initial supportive therapy came to an end.

He continued to call the therapist regularly when his spirits lagged in reaction to an interpersonal encounter with a family member and he needed a refuge—imagined or real. The session would consist of his reciting the injury and then waiting to hear the reminders of his worth and some advice that would provide the necessary support for his self. After one or two sessions, he would become invigorated and announce that he would be "calling soon"; the self-collapse again had been averted.

At this time, while his self was cohesive, the major structures were unaltered by his therapy. He continued to experience the waves of loneliness each morning and was still unable to unfold his self so as to join with his wife or anyone else to relieve his pervasive emptiness. His major mode of maintaining equilibrium was, as always, to be "Mr. Hustle." Each time the patient in therapy was invited to study his unique self/selfobject relationships with his wife and others, he reacted with anxiety and soon changed the subject—always with the rejoinder, "Hey, I have to live with her." When the therapist confronted him several times with his defense against allying himself with the therapist to study his narcissistic personality defenses, he reacted with intense anxiety and demanded to know why the therapist did not like him.

Thus he made clear that he could not enter into an alliance and study his barrier to obtaining help through his human encounters. However, he now had a permanent method of restoring equilibrium in the event of a precipitous loss of self esteem—he could call his therapist and obtain the infusions of worth to restore his equilibrium.

CASE 2. MR. J.M.

Mr. J.M., a 90-year-old man, was seen because he had told the staff at his nursing home that he no longer wished to live. He explained that he had lived long enough and that he no longer could function as the man he had been—a dentist who had practiced his profession for 45 years since his immigration to this country as a young man. He stated that his hearing was bad, that his memory was gone, that his appetite for life was gone, and that he was a useless "piece of furniture." Why should he continue? He said that he had lost his wife "some" years earlier, but it was all vague. He did not remember when he entered the home where he now resided or what the circumstances were that decided his going into the home rather than living with his surviving daughter. After telling the therapist of his intent to give up living, he thanked him for his interest and declared he had little else to say. He shifted his gaze away from the therapist, and, in effect, dismissed him.

He had come to the therapist's office in a wheelchair since walking was difficult for him, and he appeared to be withdrawn into his own inner world where no one could have an effect on\ him. In appearance, he was a small man wearing the casual clothes of a nursing-home resident; however, his grooming was perfect. He had a well-combed mane of white, wavy hair, he was closely shaven, and his nails were well kept. Beyond these details that attested to his perhaps automatic interest in himself, his posture in the wheelchair was that of a man in hibernation. This first visit was over.

He was seen again the following day, and again the

same message was delivered: "I've had enough, I'm useless." And finally, "Thank you, but I have no interest in continuing to live." On the third visit, the therapist noted observed that J.M.'s Yiddish accent had become heavier, and when he came to the "enough" part of his speech, the therapist translated it mentally into the Yiddish equivalent, *genug*, and then spoke the word. He looked at the therapist quizzically and repeated *genug*. The therapist continued in pidgin Yiddish, "Du host hat genug." He nodded and responded in Yiddish that he had been feeling that he had enough for some time. Perhaps it had started, he said, when he gave up his busy practice as a dentist in St. Louis, or perhaps when his wife died. He couldn't tell anymore. It was a long time ago. After a long interval, he looked directly at the therapist and related in Yiddish how he had entered the dental profession as a young man, after visiting and observing with interest and curiosity dentists at work in New York. Then, after working to earn his fees, he entered dental school. He had been proud to be a dentist for "all the people," as he stated in Yiddish. As he continued to relate his history, his affect became transformed into a lighter vein. When he told of his struggles to earn money and enter dental school, his tone became much more robust. He was clearly becoming more invigorated.

His statements about his immigration experiences led him to a discussion of his life in Lithuania at the turn of the century. He spoke of the family constellation and his activities as a boy until his bar mitzvah when, at age 13, he came to the United States with his family. In this overview he spoke in a mixture of Yiddish and English. The therapist was able to respond to much of it.

In the following sessions, he focused on his experiences in the past several years, during which he had lost his wife and had to give up his home. It seemed to him, he said, that he was of no value to anyone; he had done his work and wished to end his life, as he often said, "without any regrets." He mentioned that he had one daughter, whom he had visited from time to time. However, when in her home, he experienced strong waves of futility about himself and so he stopped seeing her. No place and no one gave him sufficient reason to continue living.

The empathic diagnosis seemed clear—the patient was suffering with a depleted self, a narcissistic deficit disorder. With no one did he feel mirrored, with no one did he feel invigorated. He had erected a barrier against interpersonal encounters; no one could injure him and to no one did he have to reveal his ineptitude. Vital parts of his body had been injured and deteriorated—his body strength had diminished, his hearing was poor, his brain could not compute messages from the outside nor could it construct adequate responses to the outside world. He had, as he stated, stopped reading, an activity that had been a staple of self-gratification; he had been, until "some time" ago, an avid reader of current affairs.

Next came the empathically derived therapeutic diagnosis. The patient's empathic diagnosis translated into action was designed to alleviate the distress of an acutely painful narcissistic deficit. The therapeutic diagnosis represents a program of action to diminish the self-pain. The patient's distress represented a crisis and required the therapist to "be" a selfobject functioning as a mirror, an admirer of the self that, it is to be hoped, will restore the depleted self with adequate infusions of worth.

The therapist must strive to communicate to the patient in a language, not necessarily words, from which he can recognize that he *is* of worth. Demonstrations of the therapist's admiration of the patient are what we are aiming for. At times, these communications simply take the form of regular visits during which the therapist focuses attention on the patient's unique background and demonstrates by this interest the value he or she places on the patient as a special person. At other times, the therapist brings special items—books, magazines, music cassettes—that further demonstrate the therapist's interest in the patient as a special person. Telephone calls can serve as communications of interest on weekends or holidays or at night if the patient's self-needs require this bolstering. Letters are also useful in this regard. A special function of the supportive psychotherapist of the elderly is to involve the environment in which the patients find themselves to serve in whatever selfobject function is required. In many instances, this requires the enlisting of the family or spouses to serve as sources of the mirroring or other selfobject functions that are required. Often this requires family conferences at which the patient and the spouse or family members discuss with the therapist their respective needs and their resistances to and conflicts with each other.

In the case of Mr. J.M., the therapist himself was able to lend support by functioning as a mirroring selfobject, and he also enlisted the patient's daughter to serve as an additional source of support (Weinberg, 1951).

The therapist's activities consisted of several therapeutic programs especially focused on continuing the elicitation of the patient's history, both in this country and in his country of origin. This history provided enough data so that the therapist was able to remind the patient of his considerable achievements in life. Another activity was to bring reading materials (newspapers and books) in Yiddish, which the patient and therapist read together.

The therapist was able to meet with the patient's daughter, first separately and then with the patient. She related that she had been "dismissed" by him many months earlier, perhaps six months after her mother's death as the result of a stroke. He had become morose and refused to communicate with his daughter and other family members. He had demanded to be placed in a nursing home. Once there, he had refused to let his daughter visit, and when she did so against his wishes, he would turn his back on her and refuse to communicate. She had stopped visiting two months earlier and was silently in mourning for her father, a man venerated in the family for many years.

When next the therapist met with Mr. J.M., he told him of the results of the meeting with his daughter, of which he was aware. He then asked Mr. J.M. what had led him to his "dismissal" of her. He could only relate that he no longer was a "big macher" (big or important man). The therapist then could confront him with his special shame and fear of being "a piece of furniture." Getting older, in his view, was equated with having no entitlement to any form of interest—from admiration to respect. He not only agreed with this recitation of his inner experience, but expressed the feeling that being unable to perform was being a futile person, and that he and all others of his ilk should be slaughtered as Hitler did to all the old people even before the war. The therapist continued to confront him with his views as being idiosyncratic and *not* reflecting the views of *his* family and others around him. Indeed, he was told, his daughter had been suffering because *he* had dismissed her. (Hollender, 1952; Meerloo, 1955).

After another week of regular visits he was told that it would be helpful to him and his therapy if he would visit with his daughter and the therapist. He accepted and the meeting took place. After the exchange of pleasantries, he began addressing his daughter in a gruff manner, demanding to know about "his" grandchildren. However, as she began discussing the activities of the family in great detail (with occasional tears), he became visibly softened and stopped talking from time to time simply to gaze at his daughter. The therapist then interceded and said that he felt it would be helpful to Mr. J.M. if his daughter could visit regularly. She quickly agreed, but he grumbled, "What good will it do? I'm a goner." He then moved his wheelchair away in a hostile manner, pushing aside everything in his path.

After a few days, when again approached on the same subject, he agreed to see his daughter more regularly and alluded to his previous behavior as "foolish." She began to visit regularly and his mood became more reliably in equilibrium.

Discussion

Supportive therapy for the elderly can require a mixture of environmental manipulation, an infusion of self-object supplies, and even confrontation and interpretation. The last comment reflects the observation that, in the elderly, the experience of shame about becoming "useless" serves as a potent resistance to any human encounter and so must be confronted (Goldfarb, 1955).

This clinical interaction highlights the empathic requirement of the therapist to recognize, on the level of empathic cognition, the patient's needs and capacities. Mr. J.M. was suffering from the painful admixture of neediness and the psychic barrier he had to erect against the revealing of these, to him, shameful needs. He clearly needed sustenance; after all, he could not control any part of his life. However, to him this self state of need was in no way connected with pleasure or even safety. As he said, being in the position of a dependent person to him was equated with the aged people whom Hitler had killed in 1939 because they were "useless eaters," that is, they were inferior. In his view, he was not just dependent, but he and everyone else who had to depend on others were, by definition, unacceptable to society and should not continue living. In this manner, he revealed that in his 90 years of living, one of his basic problems was that his fear of dependency had never progressed beyond his original view that it was a symptom of ineptness. His defense against the shame-filled dependency was, therefore, completely comprehensible. His defense was an archaic one, that of avoidance, since his usual defense against inadequacy, the capacity to work and overwork, was not capable of being executed by his 90-year old self (Ginzberg, 1950; Hiatt, 1972).

For the therapist, the empathic awareness of these conflicts determined the therapeutic program of action that had to be addressed. The other aspect of the diagnosis was that the therapist had to be mindful of the patient's capacity to comprehend abstract concepts, as well as of the patient's capacity to introspect and to be able to ferret out past experiences and to compare them with present experiences.

In the case of Mr. J.M., the therapist's functioning as an acceptable mirroring selfobject to him was highlighted by the ability to *respond* to his background language of Yiddish and to join with him in his native language. This Yiddish response evoked in the patient emotional responses that could be recognized and respected—his feelings of being the useless tool, the "useless eater," the "piece of furniture." It was significant that he could only—or best—reveal these inferiorities in Yiddish. Perhaps he saw the therapist's ability to recognize this language as the only acceptable way of communicating this heartfelt experience—only in Yiddish, with someone who would understand, could he unfold his pain and derive some nurturance for these experiences of painful isolation.

Armed with the data of "what" the patient was living through, the experience of inferiority, the therapist can move to try to correct the narcissistic balance problem, the narcissistic deficiency state. Mr. J.M. required from his environment an immediate dose of recognition. A feeling of inferiority is the ultimate painful experience of an absence of recognition ushering in the aloneness that is the fate of any inferior self. How to correct the narcissistic balance, the tactics of the therapy, was the problem in this case, since his 90-year-old self was not capable of using confrontations to free up his fears and defenses in order to diminish his resistance against forming a therapeutic bond. The therapist's persistence in making regular visits even when he was initially rejected was helpful in diminishing the patient's resistance to forming the therapeutic bond, as was his ability to communicate in the patient's native language.

As they continued to meet each day, he responded with more and more pleasure to the therapist's visits, which surprised the staff (Ginzberg, 1953; Oberleder, 1970). It became clear that "being" the accepting therapist without accepting *his* view of his unacceptability was of help in breaking the blockade he had established against the world. The Yiddish word *genug* ("enough") was the symbol of his disenchantment with the world. And when the therapist said that word, he looked at the therapist with a mixture of surprise and pleasure, as someone who could empathize with his self state of aloneness so that he could have some company in his nihilism.

When Mr. J.M.'s daughter was brought in, he was able to allow her to perform some selfobject functions for him and, in time, to allow her mirroring to continue to sustain him.

This supportive therapy was able to be carried out by the selfobjects—therapist and daughter—only after the initial resistance was overcome. In this clinical encounter, the resistance to the formation of the therapeutic bond—the defense transference—was mitigated not through the use of confrontations and interpretations, but through the firm, persistent leadership of the therapist.

Mr. J.M became less depressed and withdrawn and continued in this manner. He refused, however, to give up his residence in the home, and his wishes were respected.

At this writing, some nine months after the initial interviews, he has continued in equilibrium. His daughter continues to visit him in the nursing home regularly.

Chapter 6 describes psychoanalytic psychotherapy as the approach of choice for elderly patients with problems-in-living.

6

Psychoanalytic Psychotherapy

Psychoanalytic psychotherapy is the therapy of choice for those patients who have a so-called problem-in-living and for whom a major emphasis on uncovering, understanding, and neutralizing the patient-to-therapist experiences (the transference neurosis) is contraindicated. These patients have neither those pervasive self or characterological problems that ordinarily require transference analysis for relief nor a self in disarray that would require supportive psychotherapy. In these patients, ordinarily one area of self-functioning is currently a source of difficulty, an area or problem in which the therapist and the patient ally themselves to study the problem "out there" that has evoked the self-distress. The problem is one in which the special techniques of intensive psychotherapy are of help—the therapeutic bond, the confrontations to define the specific complex now on center stage, and interpretations that center on the past complex now in the present to uncover the underlying difficulty and detoxify it (Alexander & French, 1946; Dewald, 1964; Deutsch, 1949; Gill, 1954; Muslin & Val, 1987; Tarachow, 1963).

Among problems-in-living that will urge an elderly patient to seek relief with a psychotherapist may be the patient's complex reactions to an illness, to physical or mental deterioration, to a loss, or to retirement. When the psychological reactions become major experiences of anxiety or depression, the patients cannot tolerate the distress and, it is hoped, will seek or be referred for psychological treatment (Abraham, 1924b; Hiatt, 1972; Jelliffe, 1925; Peck, 1966; Safirstein, 1972; Sheps, 1955; Wayne, 1953).

The following case reports illustrate the principles of treatment and the treatment goals of psychoanalytic psychotherapy (Hiatt, 1971).

CASE 1. MR. S.T.*

When Mr. S.T. applied for treatment, he was a forlorn man in the throes of a depressive experience and unable to continue with his plan to retire at age 74. Shortly after his diagnostic interviews, when he determined not to retire immediately from his law practice, the intensive therapy began. It was clear to the patient and the therapist that the patient had to understand the genesis of his reaction to retirement; sooner or later, he would be unable to continue his present activities and thus needed to protect himself, through understanding, against future catastrophic reactions to a slowdown in his activities or to retirement.

---

*See Chapter 4, pages 67–76, for diagnostic data.

Phase 1. The Entry Into Psychotherapy and the Therapeutic Bond

In psychoanalytic psychotherapy, the bond with the patient is a crucial factor in establishing an ambience of safety in which the patient learns that the unfolding of his or her self issues evokes only interest and attempts at understanding at the patient's pace and with the patient's changing capacities in mind. The next task is learning *the basic rule* of psychotherapy: the patients' assignment is to reveal all of their thoughts, feelings, and sensations, even as they experience the intrapsychic pressure of shame, anxiety, or guilt militating against disclosure (Freud, 1912b, 1913).

In working with the elderly, the task of establishing and maintaining the ambience of safety is an important and sometimes difficult one for the therapist since it involves continuous monitoring of the patient's mental and somatic capacities throughout the entire course of the therapy.

Another important facet of the therapy is the flexibility required of the therapist; at times, the psychotherapy "work" will be an entire session devoted solely to the supportive therapy tactics of selfobject calming and to offering advice, or it will be an entire session of ventilation of rage inspired by an "insult" from, for example, a relative or a store clerk. At other times, the psychotherapy work will be devoted in part to a discussion of the current movies in town. In these instances, when the patient's needs are to gain "transference gratifications" or, more simply, to gain a human response, the patients reveal that their appetites for here-and-now gratifications are compelling—they are lonely, they need calming, they need direction. At still other times, the patient may be too enervated somatically and mentally for the work of psychotherapy and cannot study his or her inner experiences and perform the other necessary tasks, such as ferreting out early experiences and synthesizing these early experiences with the present reality. When the patient realizes that the work proceeds at the patient's pace and without criticism, the ambience of safety is ensured.

The therapeutic bond is of special importance in therapy with the elderly. This bond in psychoanalytic psychotherapy refers to the positive transference with the therapist, a continuing source of mirroring and calming–soothing–direction giving. The therapeutic bond offers the patient a source of support and is not to be disturbed by focusing on its derivatives as a transference from earlier relationships that would undermine its current functioning as a source of worth or direction. In psychoanalytic therapy, it is destined to be a silent transference configuration of psychotherapy.

With the elderly, as with others from other age groups, the formation of the therapeutic bond commonly has to go through stages of "experimentations." These experimental trials, from the patient's side, contain the elements of establishing a relationship of trust with a stranger, who often is younger. The elderly person has to determine whether this stranger can "tolerate" being a caretaker to a person, the patient, who looks as though he or she should be the caretaker. The tactics of these experimentations are a collection of trial balloons commonly sent up by all patients, of course, to determine the therapist's coolness under fire: rebukes, silences, challenges, interruptions, supercilious behaviors, and frequent reminders of age differences.

Here are vignettes from the initial therapeutic sessions with Mr. S.T.

Therapist: How are you? As I told you, we're going to see each other two times a week. Just speak freely of your activities during the week, but be careful to say everything that comes into your mind —thoughts, feelings, sensations. If you learn to speak freely without restraint, important underlying experiences will emerge that will help us to understand your current reactions.

I also want you to know that at times I won't say much because I don't want to interfere with your thoughts.

Mr. S.T.: I understand. (*shoulders droop; looks at the floor*) I'm tired. I had a lousy week. You see, I've always—foolishly, I'm sure—prized my memory. Colleagues and judges for 40 years would marvel at my ability to come up with those tiny details in a piece of law that make all the difference in a court of law or a judge's chambers. Well, it's all gone now! I've always heard that the first sign of senility is the old memory box going down the tube. This week it happened. Now I know I'm beyond repair. On the surface, it's of no importance, but some young man asked me for a reference, a court decision in an area that I've always known quite well. I just went blank—the memory is gone. I've always been so used to a head filled with thoughts that connect one area to another. Gone. Gone. (*shoulders droop again*) I've had it. (*eyes fill with tears*)

Therapist: (*after a long pause*)It's so difficult for you to feel compassion for yourself when you're not up to par.

Mr. S.T.: (*arousing himself as if from a stupor*) Did I understand you to say that I don't feel compassion for myself when I'm an old fool? That's right! I don't feel compassion or respect or kindly toward myself as I turn into an old fool. I saw their faces when I couldn't come up with that court decision; they all looked away. Well, we at least all agree that an old man should be cut off. You're right, I don't feel compassion or respect nor am I sorry for me-as-fool. This is not the way I want to leave the planet. And she can't stand me when I'm in trouble either. I don't blame her, for all those years—35 years—I was Mr. Responsible. She, too, looks at me with a tension since I've been moping around. What in the world would she do after I'm gone? I already pay all the bills, organize everything about our lives, including the vacations. You know, I made a bad mistake. I told her this week of my memory trouble. She made a snide remark about me getting "dotty," she called it. I got out of the room in a hurry. It hit me in the gut, like someone actually hit me. I certainly know where I stand with her when I get more tired and more out of it.

What did you say I showed? Oh yes, no compassion for myself when I goof up. That's right. Compassion, that's a bunch of crap. (*quiet for two minutes*)

Therapist: I guess what we're looking at here is the special feeling you have for yourself when you're not performing at a high level. And, therefore, there must be quite a difference between the way you value yourself when you're on top as contrasted with the demeaning or anxiety you experience when you're not, in your view, on top.

The early stages of intensive psychotherapy are taken up with the attempt to illuminate the "what" of the initial phase of therapy. Essentially, the therapist and patient attempt to unearth the dominant experience of the patient that constitutes the major aspect of the current psychic dilemma. Whether it constitutes a transference position or an underdeveloped part of the self, the therapist and patient struggle to uncover the crucial self state that is now in focus in all of its meanings. Thus, in Mr. S.T., the "what," the phenomenological experience that causes him anguish, is the experience of a self in a state of weakness that is associated not with succor or benevolent guidance, but only with despair.

After many confrontations with the fact of his unique experience of his slowed-down-brain, the patient could finally "see" the associations he made between imperfections—errors, forgetfulness, *and* ignominy. Therapist and patient could now move to the second research question in psychotherapy: Where does it come from? The psychotherapy proceeds to an uncovering of the unique experiences that ushered in (in this case) the equation of imperfections with rejection or hatred. Whatever the initial phase revealed as the central experience to be worked on, a conflict or a developmental defect, the second phase is of necessity directed to uncovering the fixations that will form the interpretations of the third phase. Another segment of a session in transition between the first and second phases was as follows:

Mr. S.T.: All of a sudden I'm preoccupied with little worries—money, my health, my social life—and the dumb thing is I express these concerns to her. Now my wife is not the gal you open up to with your concerns. She goes ape. What a mistake, what a mistake. She said to me things I would hit a man for. (*sad; one minute of silence*) She really knows how to hit. "Why are you telling me these things? You never told me I had anything to worry about with money. What kind of a man are you, coming home to tell me about these things? Go dump on your family. I gave you the best years of my life. Why are you making my life so miserable? How could you do this to me? You never had any respect for me, just come home and dump!" Then she runs out crying, screaming that I'm a wimp and no one else but her could have lived with me all these years. And then the inevitable references to my mother and my sister. She would never overlook an opportunity to knock my mother and my sister. "Your mother never had any use for you either, she knew what you were. She favored your sister because she knew what you were." And on and on. I never have been able to tell her my troubles. I'm down, I'm on my own. She's not all that bad. I just can't tell her anything, and I seldom do.

Sometimes I let it out and then the inevitable happens.

Therapist: Once again, we're looking at this experience of yours when you feel needy or down or weak. Suddenly you're uneasy or ashamed or running away. This time it came out with your wife. It's clear that she has a special reaction to you when you get down, but it's also clear that when you get down, it leaves you hopeless.

Mr. S.T.: Yeah, you're right. I feel hopeless—it *is* hopeless. At least that's the way I feel.

Therapist: We've seen this complex now many times. It's been a central experience you're having *now*, but it's been there a long time, that's my hunch. Where's it coming from? How did this get started that each time you need help it's frightening?

Mr. S.T.: But Doctor, she *does* explode each time I approach her with my problems. (*tearful*) It's no joke. Each time I want to tell her something special about me, I'm in hot water. I'm telling you, the woman's a terror.

At this juncture, the patient has not yet effected a "therapeutic split" sufficiently to self-observe his self-of-inferiority as differentiated from his ordinary interpersonal view of the world, "the woman's a terror." The reference to the wife's power is as if *she* were responsible for his special feelings of inferiority when he is needy, rather than his unique intrapsychic response whenever he experiences neediness. He, of course, is and always has been free to dismiss her comments, to dismiss her and seek other sources of comfort, yet he not only stays with her, but he succumbs to her anger and becomes uneasy. He has "pedestalized" her and her words; at this moment, he is not free to leave or dismiss her or to do combat with her. The therapist must make more confrontations until the patient "sees" his entry into this unique experience of the self-of-inferiority establishing a relationship with an authority figure who, on the surface, offers no comfort and in front of whom he feels hopeless, anxious, and apologetic.

Therapist: I understand *her* reactions but it's important for you to see that whenever she expresses these critical comments, *you* cave in—like she's "right" or she's got the power. It's never, "I'm needy," with the self-assurance that your wants are legitimate. You're a different man when you're needy than when you're wheeling and dealing at the office.

Mr. S.T.: Yeah, I guess so. Yeah, I guess I understand. I never say to Alice: "You don't meet me halfway." I guess I get nervous when she comes on strong. Why can't she bend? She's so tough. Gee, I feel so bad again, like the way I did when I first came here. Being old is not fun, I hate it. I want to say the hell with it all and just go! When I'm at the office, people ask all day, "What can I get you?" or "Do you need something?" or "could you please advise me about this or that?" At home, it's like I put on a new set of clothes, a butler's suit. It's ridiculous, but the minute she starts that first barrage, I wilt or melt. I just know I feel lost and I'm fighting for my life, but I know I've already lost.

Of course, retirement would mean an endless barrage of this kind of stuff. Oh my! (*long silence*)

Once again, he slipped into the interpersonal or social/psychological view: she "makes" him valueless. To alter his self state would mean in his view that *she* had to imbue him with worth. She was, at that moment, the identified purveyor of worth—and only if he exhibited certain behaviors. For example, in his view, she would never give him affirmation for just being "around the house" (retirement) without, at the same time, being of service to her. She rewarded only those achievements and activities that were carried out on her behalf; she would not reward a man at home who was reflective or self-serving.

And so, at this point, Mr. S.T.'s capacity to study the depths of his inner experience with regard to his spouse was limited and had to be encouraged sufficiently to enable him to "see" the particular self state he enters into with his wife. Once he could self-observe this unique self and dissect it from the rest of his persona, he and the therapist could trace it to the self/selfobject dyad from which it emanated. The therapist's focus at this stage of the therapy was to continue to encourage the patient to recognize his special experiences with his wife so that he could ultimately be in touch with the intrusion into his persona of the special self of his childhood that was holding center stage.

Phase 2. The Investigation of the Past

At a later date in the therapy, the following material emerged.

Mr. S.T.: Hi, I'm feeling a little bit more lighthearted. I guess I'm feeling young at heart, as the song goes, because I told the wife we should go out of town for this coming weekend. Naturally, she threw cold water on the project. *(quiet for a short time)* She still gets to me, but less so. So what can I tell you, I become putty in her hands, but less so. What you say is true. I've got to grab myself when she starts her diatribes. This time it was, "How could you talk about vacation in one breath, and in the next talk about cutting expenses?" Ah, hell!

Therapist: There really are two parts of this experience of yours in focus: one, the view of her that you experience—*suddenly* you experience her words as commands—and the view of yourself, the subservient one that you become.

Mr. S.T.: Yep, yep, yep. Isn't that tragic? But it's true and it's been true. I don't remember when it wasn't true in our relationship. And just about nowhere else. But with this retirement—it's a big deal—all that time with her. Retirement means, you know, travel with her, golf with her, dinner with her, TV with her, bridge with her. And now I guess you're telling me I've got to toughen myself up against her.

Therapist: Well, it really is this, you find yourself entering into a special self around her—a self of weakness. That's what makes you feel you have to be tough, as if you have to fight off her power, but it really is to overcome the weakened self you *become* around her.

Mr. S.T.: You know, it's not always there. At times, I

feel calm and self-assured, but of course it's usually when I'm directing traffic. But you're right. When I have to turn to her for me, I'm a fool. You know—affection, sex, that kind of stuff.

At this juncture, the data revealed that the patient was now able to dissect the transferential self he experienced from the total persona so as to examine it with the therapist. After many of these instances in which it was clear that the patient had "seen" the transferential self, the therapy was ready to move to the second research query of psychotherapy: Where does this self or anxiety or wish come from? The second research query is the investigation of the background material that has determined the vulnerabilities and patterns of the patient being examined. This investigation, the application of the so-called genetic point of view of psychoanalysis, is of special importance in uncovering the *fixations* in the development of patients that continue to have an impact on their current lives. The therapist—once the data reveal that the patient is now aware of the transference configuration or unique affect or disarray that constitutes the essential element in his or her difficulties—is now enabled to initiate the investigation into the second phase of the therapy: Where does this (self state, affect, etc.) come from?

Therapist: This experience you have around your wife of becoming weak and anxious, where does it come from? Can you remember situations or times in your background when you showed this pattern?

Of what does it remind you? What does this becoming weak to a person stir up in you?

Mr. S.T.: (*quiet, saddened; sighs a few times*) Well, I'll tell
you this. I never met a person quite like my wife.
We did have a lot of trouble back when I was growing up. I had an older sister who was trouble
spelled with a capital "T." Boy, she was a handful
to all of us. Ever since I can remember, she was
trouble. I don't remember me crying, but I sure
remember her caterwauling from day to night. My
mother and father, and I too, were caught up all
day in keeping her cooled off. I guess today you'd
call her a spastic kid or hyperkinetic or as having
an attention-deficit problem. She was always just
tearing around and tracing around. It seems like
she also had polio when I was an infant and had
to be hospitalized. Well, anyway, my mother certainly had her hands full, but not with me. I was
one of those good kids, in school, in church, you
know. My father, he was too busy; he was a
butcher, and he always seemed to be the kind of
quiet guy you never notice. We went fishing every
now and then. Oh yeah, we slept together, he and
I, a lot because it seems my sister needed to be
with my mother. It always seemed to be that my
mother leaned on me, especially to go with my
sister, you know, kind of like her escort, to the
movies, to the library. I always resented it because
everyone made fun of me because I couldn't play
ball if I had to go with her, and also she acted
goofy. Like she never could walk straight or run or
ride a bike. Years later, I understood it was because

of her brain troubles, but I was just always embarrassed to be with her and she refused to go with
my mother to those places because it embarrassed
her. I was tall, so I looked older. She was four years
older—and once, just once, I *had* to go to a high-
school dance with her. It was awful, her giggling
and being unable to keep in time with the music
and every once in a while just walking off the floor,
leaving me looking like a dunce! Next time my
mother asked me, I ran away from home for the
night. I guess I kind of grew up by myself; they
were always so busy and scared by her outbursts.
I guess they finally found a doctor who prescribed
some drug, and I don't know how she is now because I haven't contacted her since my folks passed
away; that's been like 30 years.

I guess it took me a long time to get over those
people. I discovered I had a brain in high school
and I got interested in things in books. I had a
couple of teachers interested in me, and so on. In
the service, I did O.K. too. I was in North Africa
when we went into what was then called Palestine,
an exciting time. When I got out and went to law
school, I guess I was still a stiff person and didn't
go out much. I finally got married when I was
nearly 40. Well, she really popped the question.
We met at one of those church-sponsored dances.
She looked real good to me. I guess I was backward
about things like compatibility factors. I guess I
thought all marriages work out. I also suppose I
was lonely; I'd been working all my life and she
did flatter me a lot in those early days. In fact, I

never did have anybody else flatter me a lot. My mother was always proud of me when I did well in school, and, of course, I supported my parents for a long while before they died. Just before I started going heavy with my wife, they both died. He had a heart attack and she had a stroke within a year of his death. I know I paid my dues, but I never felt I did. I still can feel, if I think about it, that she had a tough life and I had it pretty easy. I got to go on to school without even paying for it; she had it *so* hard.

Therapist: So with your mother you had to be *her* source of support. This she valued in you.

Mr. S.T.: On yeah. You got it. (*chuckles*) I was always the good kid. Of course, it helped me out a lot in later years; no one ever had to tell me to study or to stay up to write a brief. I don't know why I feel so sad now. (*silence, teary*)

Therapist: My hunch is you felt sad lots of times as a kid because when you were scared or needy, you knew you had nowhere to go. It was futile.

Mr. S.T.: You got it. We were all working to keep my sister quiet. But tell me, what good does it do now to drag up these things? They're all gone, and I've already had my life. She couldn't help herself and so, what the hell, I learned to get along without a lot of things. I was always so good at doing without. I'm a do-without expert. I could always get along with doing an extra shift wherever I went—school, army, you name it.

Therapist: And so you learned two things: first, to be of service, which gave you rewards from your people;

and secondly, to stay *far away* from showing need. Actually, it was more important than anything else to stay away from being needy. That you've always been frightened of displaying or revealing.

In his associations to his background over many sessions, Mr. S.T. was able to unfold the elements of his background—being caught up in a web of subservience to a mother whose mirroring was so selectively attached to his gifts to her. However, the most crucial element in his background was the genesis of his phobia of dependency. Mr. S.T. became phobic over revealing to anyone the self of need, always anticipating a dangerous outcome, a dangerous response to his expression of need. This was, of course, the core of his reenactment with his spouse and of his resistance to aging. His fear of becoming the needy elderly person was, by transference (displacement) logic, the reinstitution of the needy youngster in a relationship in which revealing need was equivalent to rejection. The extent of the danger is difficult to approximate empathically since it involved the therapist's empathic capacity here to read himself into the self of a youngster whose fear of his mother's rejection was overwhelming. Since it was always in short supply, her mirroring was experienced as a precious commodity. Further, the fear of being *without* any mirroring and/or idealized parent presence—to be totally alone as an infant, as a needy youngster—is a source of danger that is not easily forgotten. Being needy, and so evoking this frightening self state, had to be avoided at all costs for Mr. S.T., who had spent a lifetime reinforcing himself against any sign of dangerous dependency.

Unfolding the dangerous dependency would remind him of when he was totally alone, but more important, a time when he was totally unable to sustain himself. Revealing his dependency was tantamount to initiating a panic we can only partially comprehend.

After many interactions along the same lines over several months, the therapist began the work of interpreting Mr. S.T.'s dilemma in accordance with the data that had been unearthed.

Phase 3. The Working-Through Phase: What Is This Complex Doing in Your Current Life?

The therapist's task in this last stage of therapy is to encourage the patient to establish the crucial connection between the unearthed data from the past and to relate the data to the current experience. The past-in-the-present often, or most often, involves a limitation or interference with the here-and-now life of the patient. And so, armed with the material of the past, the therapist could proceed to help free this patient from the shackles of the past by illuminating his unconscious feelings toward his wife and his unconscious fears of becoming elderly.

The following are segments of an interview in this phase of psychoanalytic psychotherapy.

Mr. S.T.: Well, this week was a bummer. She really got on me and I really took it on the chin. I couldn't wait to get here to put this on the table so we could understand it. (*smiles*) I was watching a ball game on Saturday afternoon and fell asleep sometime in the middle of the game. I guess it was boring. I was awakened by this screaming hyena: "What are you doing to me?' You know that the play starts at eight o'clock and you're not dressed! You're going to get me all upset! Where have you been hiding? You do this to me all the time." That was for openers. *Then* she let me have it! She dragged up crap from the past that I told her about my mother paying attention to my sister and denying me. But she used that against me. She said, "No one has ever liked you, you're unlikable." But I wasn't laughing; it got me so down. I couldn't laugh. I couldn't dismiss her. I couldn't put her down. She got to me. (*saddened look; quiet*)

Therapist: All of a sudden, her words were not those of your wife. They were the words of a tyrannical authority figure, withdrawing her love, leaving you all alone, again. Nothing to laugh at.

Mr. S.T.: You're right. I couldn't tell her to go fly a kite. This happens to me so often around her. Maybe that's why I remember all the words she says. I bet she can't remember one word I've ever said. Well, there you have it—my wife, the big shot. I never thought it would happen to me. You know, before I got married, I was looked up to at the club I went to. I was—the word they used in those days— "sharp." I mean, I was looked up to by both men and women. Now here I am, reduced to a guy who goes around quoting his wife. (*saddened*)

This last reference, with the addition of the diminished affect, revealed that again the patient had entered into the self state of futility, of the youngster who never expects that his "magna mater" will attempt to understand him or to cherish his longings and strivings. The therapist's task now, after the initial confrontation, was to *interpret* the material along the lines of the mother–wife–patient similarities so that the patient might "see" the transference he was effecting of mother onto wife and of the youngster he was onto his current self.

Therapist: What we're looking at here is your experiencing your wife in a manner similar to the way you experienced your mother. Once again, you're into that experience of looking up to the "boss" and you have suddenly become the youngster. Her words are not those of a peer but the words of a queen talking to one of her subjects. Her opinion of what you're doing is the only important opinion; if she said you're doing something absurd, it *is* absurd.

An interpretation, in contrast to a confrontation, does not round up manifest data in order to offer to the patient an observation or a hypothesis. An interpretation goes beyond the manifest data to offer a hypothesis pertaining to unconscious strivings. The interpretation given here was a transference interpretation based on the genetic material uncovered. To determine whether an interpretation is valid or not, the therapist must follow the subsequent associations. Whether or not the patient acquiesces to the therapist's comments does not establish the validity of the interpretation.

Interpretations and their sequelae constitute the main behaviors during this phase of therapy. The interpretations initiate the working-through process in which the cycle of the past-to-present illuminations takes place. The material of the present-day interactions—in this case, the unusual experience the patient had of his wife—which reveal the past conflicts or deficits or fixations, is now connected by the therapist with those special experiences of the past so as to demonstrate these connections or reveal that the patient experiences the present interaction with the same expectations or fear or hatred the patient had in the past situation.

After sufficient interpretations, the working-through process should eventuate in enough illumination of the patient's main sector of difficulty to allow the patient freedom from the past entanglements. The patient's awareness becomes manifest as an awareness of the wish before it becomes action. The patient will say, "I felt I should quietly walk away, but I realized that was an old piece of business, an old way to get along." And so the patient, recognizing the old patterns, can begin to isolate the old patterns without being deflected from the strivings of a mature self.

After the interpretation in this case ("You're experiencing your wife in a manner similar to the way you experienced your mother; you're into that experience of looking up to the 'boss' and you have suddenly *become* the youngster"), the therapist follows the associations to determine the validity of the interpretation.

Mr. S.T.: Well yeah, she's the boss, but you mean that I put her on a throne like she was a big shot. Like my mom, you said. Huh! Well I always did try to please my mom. I guess I was always sensitive to what she wanted me to be or do—that's true. Was my mom a boss? I never thought about it that way. I never told her any problems of mine, you know. I mean *never*. She was, as he was, so consumed with my sister's craziness. I certainly ran home when my mom wanted me, ran away from ball games and everything. But I always thought I wanted to please her. I never thought I was frightened of her. Of course, I could never complain to her or criticize her. You mean I was not just trying to please her, that I was frightened to do otherwise? That I *had* to please her or else? Or else what? My mother reject *me*? Huh? I certainly could not go against her. I certainly could never let her know of problems, just good stuff. That's what she wanted to hear, just good stuff.

At this stage, the patient could not make the crucial connections between his current self-experience and his past self-experience as well as could be expected since he could not yet unearth the fear of abandonment by his mother. At a later stage, he was able to remember more incidents that disclosed the fears of desertion that were involved in his interactions with her.

Mr. S.T.: You know, when you pointed out the submission to and the pedestalizing, as you call it, of my wife and the similarity to my life at home, I remembered an episode of me being *scared* at home, in fact, a couple of episodes.

I was working by the time I was 7 years old, delivering flowers, papers, bakery goods. I kept a part of the money and gave the rest to my mother. I was saving up secretly for a bike. It took me a couple of years, but then one day I brought this dumb old black bike from the Salvation Army Store. They sold everything in those stores. When I came home with it, my mother looked at me and didn't talk to me for three days. I felt terrible. I was 12 and I thought that I had done something terrible. She started talking to me again after a couple of days, but we never discussed that bike again. I took it to my friend's house and I used it sometimes. I guess she thought I'd start being a bad kid or something. A couple of years later, I saved up to buy a fancy shirt. When I brought that shirt home, she just looked past me and I got frightened again, like she had left me. I never knew what made her angry at me. She sometimes criticized me for not watching my money or spending too much.

The more I talk about what went on at home, the more I remember her. She really spent a lot of time in bed. I guess she had a lot of sick headaches or something, but I remember lots of times when she went to bed at six o'clock, my father was away somewhere, my sister was out, and I was alone a lot at night. It wasn't so bad, but there certainly wasn't a lot of special attention to me; whatever they had, my sister got it. I guess I learned early to keep my own counsel. My mother certainly wasn't bothered by me like my sister bothered her. My sister never seemed to worry about bothering

them, but I always was uneasy about bothering
her.
   I guess I kind of see the connection. If my mother
wanted me, I'd be there quick! When my wife starts
talking, I'm almost at attention, like I'm uneasy
about what directives I will have to obey. It is never
a peerlike relationship, a man to a woman.
Therapist: If you open up to her, ultimately she'll go off
and leave you like your mother did, physically and
psychologically. You are sensitive to the threat of
separation in any form, such as divorce.

   As the working through proceeded, the patient's remembrances revealed instances in which his inner experiences were those of fear that his mother would desert
him. In the early part of his therapy, when first queried
about his views of his mother's relatedness to him, his
comments were that she was "always there." As the
therapy proceeded, the early views of her were shown
to be a mixture of the defenses of denial and reaction
formation. His mother's support was revealed as
attached to selective mirroring of her positive reactions
to his achievements and exemplary behaviors. As the
therapy continued, the evidence of his "fear" of not
being perfect was revealed. It became clear that he had
been frightened that she would desert him. He always
ran home lest she run away from him, since he had
learned early in life that she wouldn't be immediately
available—for him the basic trust was a limited trust.
Other memories of her not mirroring his great achievements as a youngster in saving to buy a bicycle or arti-
cles of clothing were screen memories, selfobject screen

memories. Similar to screen memories in general, the retained memory (the screen) represents a headline under which many similar memories—in this case, of absent or deficient or too-selective mirroring—are contained. In his experience, *this* selfobject (and her clones in his total life experience) was as rare and as precious as any rare element and had to be catered to and supported lest she be blown away. Therefore, it was imperative that she view him in a positive manner and that he perform any action necessary to earn her gratitude since the only reassurance he might obtain that she would not leave would be that she was not angry or critical of him. He needed these reassurances that she would not leave since he had been subject since birth to a mother and father who left him often, either to attend to a clamoring sister or to go to bed. The behaviors of being the good, clean, quiet, little and big boy were adaptations to maintain the self/selfobject dyad in a positive balance, without rancor or separation.

Mr. S.T.: My mother was always there. (*quiet; cries*) No she wasn't. Even when my sister was not there, she was really into herself and really a negative person.

One of the tragic vicissitudes of living with deficient selfobject is the self-deficiencies that will result when the selfobject deficiency is in the infusion of mirroring—the affirmation experiences that caretakers provide that become internalized as the abiding experience of self-worth. Another deficiency that results when a caretaker is inadequate is that of missing the strength that comes with an adequate experience of an idealized self-object whose power rubs off on the infant self when there is sufficient contact with this power broker, the idealized figure of one's infancy and childhood. The functions this selfobject provides throughout childhood are first to calm and soothe, and then to offer directions and control, later to offer values to serve as compasses for one's life.

When this patient was in elementary school, his self was not an inflated one of a self with adequate *esteem* nor was it filled with the vigor of a self that has had adequate merging with the strength of an idealized self-object. He was overaccommodating, overinhibited, and frightened of criticism.

As the interpretations continued of the present understood through the past, the patient's capacity to extricate himself from the reenacted self/selfobject fixation was enhanced. A later segment is as follows:

Mr. S.T.: Something's happened. My wife's buzzing has become less of a problem. I can't tell you when it happened. It just did. She started to be pissy about the time of an event, a bridge game. I was too late or we wouldn't get there on time or whatever. Suddenly, at least in retrospect, I did not rush to my defense but I suddenly saw a nervous person, kind of hysterical, and so I made the usual signs with my hands of calming and dismissal. She started to come on strong about a relative and once again got vituperative. I listened and again I looked at her. It's funny, all these years of being pushed around. I almost started to laugh, but checked it. Who the hell am I laughing at, after all?

Phase 4. The Termination Phase in Psychoanalytic Psychotherapy

Although the termination phase is an especially important aspect of all therapies, it is specially important in psychotherapy with the elderly, in whom there is so much loss to which they must adapt. Therefore, the therapist is called upon to perform the delicate mission of finishing up the work of the therapy without terminating the relationship, albeit it, of course, will be altered. First, the therapist and patient, *agreeing* that there has been symptom reduction and that considerable work has been done on the *understanding* of the symptoms, decide that the number of sessions can be decreased. Second, the therapist makes clear to the patient that their relationship is an important way to maintain psychological equilibrium and so should be continued in some form to be dictated by the patient's needs. One model would be to meet monthly for "a while" and after a couple of months to evaluate whether to meet every other month or continue to meet each month. A segment from the final phase of psychotherapy in the case of Mr. S.T. is as follows:

Mr. S.T.: I understand that we can cut down since I really do feel better and I'm understanding more and more of my relationship with my wife. Do we have to? I'm doing well. Well, I guess you mean I should try it on my own now. I should fly myself for a while because I can fly by myself with your endorsement.

Therapist: Right, but I believe we should continuue to see each other once a month for a time and see how you're doing. Then we'll check to see how things are going. If everything is O.K. at that point, we'll continue to see each other regularly.

Mr. S.T.: Well, I guess I should be pleased, but I'm not. I mean, it's sad. At my station in life, who the hell wants to lose anyone or anything?

Thus a so-called termination for some elderly patients might be, as with younger patients, without the addition of the attention to the continuation of the relationship; for others, it is as described above. Therefore, after the first year of the slowdown of the sessions, some patients may make it clear that they want to fly alone (with the therapist's blessings) and check in if they are in need. Others value the slowdown and do not wish a precipitous rupture of the bond.

The *outcome* result of psychoanalytic psychotherapy with the elderly is difficult to evaluate in comparison with the results obtained in psychotherapy with younger patients. The forming of a therapeutic alliance, the working-through phase, the uncovering of the crucial genetic material all take longer in the elderly, but the benefits are important to those elderly patients who experience their lives differently.

Over the next several months, as Mr. S.T. terminated his intensive psychotherapy, he continued to experiment with his programs of independent activity. Each time he would experience a rush of anxiety and revisit his fears of being displeasing—in his view—to the magna mater in his present and past lives. In this way, he became able to isolate this childhood self/selfobject pattern from the rest of his self.

The termination of intensive psychotherapy for all patients of all ages comes about when the problem for which the patient sought help is overcome or sufficiently reduced so as no longer to be a problem. The termination period is ordinarily a short one relative to that when an analysis ends, and so it is with the elderly patients.

However, for the elderly, the concept of termination does not constitute an end to the relationship. In the ending of a psychotherapy with an elderly patient, the therapist announces that the therapy is now to go into another phase, that of maintenance therapy in which the patient meets with the therapist on a much more limited basis—from twice a week to twice a month, and then once a month, and then diminishing as required. In some instances, this will be three or four times a year and in others once or twice a year, with each case to be evaluated separately.

With the elderly, perhaps more than with any other group of patients, the therapist must continue to support the "new" structures that have developed in psychotherapy. The "new" pole of assertiveness, the "new" pole of values—all these "new" acquisitions so precious to the self. Therefore, the therapist, in maintaining contact with the patient, will serve to sustain these gains and to help the patient to stay free of the intrusions of the past.

At this juncture, one could ask: What is unique about

the intensive psychotherapy treatment approach for the elderly? What is different in the psychoanalytic psychotherapy for the elderly? A related query is: Of what value is it to advise this complex and difficult work for elderly people?

The therapist advises intensive psychotherapy for an elderly person when the patient's self-cohesiveness will benefit from the insight gained into a discrete problem area with which the patient is struggling. The therapeutic diagnosis of intensive psychotherapy for an elderly patient is perhaps made too infrequently, although not for the reasons Freud (1905, 1924) gave at the turn of the century, that in the elderly, "the elasticity of the mental processes is as a rule lacking." It is this author's suspicion, however, and one shared by many, that the psychological distresses of the elderly are not sufficiently addressed through advising psychotherapy (Hollender, 1952; Meerloo, 1955). It is also his view, without any other than anecdotal evidence to back it up, that what psychotherapy is performed for the elderly is usually for a crisis in the patient's self. Moreover, to conduct a careful set of diagnostic interviews and advise the proper modality to fit the patient's distress should become the norm for our psychotherapy of the elderly. The therapy chosen—support, uncovering, psychoanalysis—should fit the patient's empathic diagnosis, as well as the patient's credentials for the therapy chosen. If the patient has psychological needs for intensive psychotherapy and has the self-credentials to perform the work, the capacity for trust and for self-observing, then he or she should begin the uncovering psychotherapy without delay.

Apart from the regular attention to the patient's physiological status, there are other unique aspects of the uncovering work with the elderly. These differences are difficult to generalize and, therefore, difficult to present for purposes of standardization and research. However, a number of psychotherapists of the elderly have commented on some of these qualities (Gitelson, 1948; Hiatt, 1972; Hollender, 1952), which will be described in the following section.

The therapist of the elderly must be prepared to be patient with the rate of psychotherapeutic progress; repeated confrontations and interpretations are the rule until the therapist has acquired evidence that a given confrontation has enabled the patient to "see," for example, a transference configuration that is important. The therapist also must be patient if the person demonstrates the need to "run away" for a time during the sessions by turning the discussion to mundane matters. The titration of the confrontations and interpretations so as to avoid overloading of the self with shame or anxiety is important in the psychotherapy of any patient, and particularly for the elderly. Instead of pursuing the avoidance, as one would with a younger person, accepting the flight is often the proper therapeutic posture. Similar advice holds for transference interpretations; they are to be utilized *only* when there is significant defense transference that requires an interpretation. The elderly patient is in dire need, as a rule, of maintaining a therapeutic bond, a positive transference, which is always weakened by transference interpretations.

The therapist must be alert to the need for the techniques and postures of the supportive therapy approaches. In the elderly, the needs for direction and mirroring emerge in any modality. There are also losses with which these patients struggle—a death, an economic fear or hardship, a rebuff or disappointing attitude on the part of relatives or friends, and the omnipresent fear of some manifestation of deterioration in the special senses, the musculature, or the musculoskeletal system. Flexibility is the key to the psychotherapist of the elderly. A sad or tearful elderly patient is to be comforted in a manner that is acceptable to the therapist.

The termination of a psychotherapeutic process with an elderly person is reached when the presenting complex is neutralized or removed from the patient's psyche. However, as stated, the need for the relationship is often still present. The patient should be told that the meetings will continue, although on a less frequent basis. But the patient should also be advised that the therapist is available for telephone calls or meetings at any time between the scheduled meetings and would prefer that the patient call if there is any psychic distress or if the patient simply wants to make contact out of loneliness.

CASE 2. MS. A.K.

Ms. A.K., a 74-year-old retired nurse, came to therapy for diagnosis and treatment of her anxiety attacks, which began, as she remembered, on a trip with her cousin and longtime house mate to Mexico. Her 75-year-old cousin, who was also retired, had been a physician. On this particular trip, one of many they had taken over the past five years of retirement for both of them, it became clear that Ms. A.K.'s cousin had signs and symptoms of severe cardiovascular disease. The mild angina that she had previously suffered was now intruding on her with any manifestation of affect. Ms. A.K. traced her anxiety and depression to this event. However, she first went to her internist, complaining of memory loss and with it her fear that she had Alzheimer's disease. She was frightened that no one in her house would be able to care for her if she became more regressed and that she would be institutionalized. When she was told that she had no organic brain deficits, she, in her words, "collapsed" and became agitated and began weeping uncontrollably. She was then referred for psychological treatment.

In her initial sessions, she was still preoccupied with concerns over her mentational functions, especially her recall of words. However, she did discuss in detail the precipitating events of her disequilibrium and with it the history of her relationship with her longtime friend and cousin, with whom she had lived since her nursing college days in an East Coast city. Ms. A.K.'s entire relationships in life had been centered on her cousin since leaving her family of origin after boarding school.

Ms. A.K.'s father and mother were into the "religious life," he as a minister and she as the minister's wife and a teacher. Ms. A.K. had been essentially an only child. A younger brother, three years her junior was born with a congenital heart condition. He died at the age of 2, when she was 5 years old. She described her mother as a hardworking person who seemed always to be "somewhere else," cleaning and polishing and "setting things straight." She also revealed that there was little in the way of touching in her childhood; she seemed to become an adult early in life. Her mother and father often read to her, and she herself learned to read at the age of 3. Prayers and theological instruction were important experiences as well. Her father, also hardworking, was devoted to his ministry and the usual service life of a small-town cleric. He was described as more emotional than his wife; he smiled and laughed more and could cry when appropriate. He too, like his spouse, valued orderliness and regularity and mirrored Ms. A.K.'s intellectual prowess, which apparently was recognized as substantial early in her life.

When she finished elementary school, her father arranged for a scholarship to a boarding school in an adjacent state but several hundred miles away. She cried, but silently, when informed that she was to go since the education there would be superior to that offered by any school in their vicinity. Her entry into boarding school at the age of 12 basically marked the end of her physical contact with her parents, who soon after left the United States to become missionaries at their church's mission in Africa. They saw their daughter only twice during her teenage years, and when she was 16, both parents died in Africa during an outbreak of dysentery. She continued in boarding school until she went to live with her mother's sister. Her aunt's daughter (Ms. A.K.'s cousin) and Ms. A.K. began their relationship at this time, which continued when Ms. A.K. went to nursing school and her cousin to medical school in the same medical center. Neither seemed to have any need for other people. While their relationship was always "close," there was no sexual aspect to their union. They shared the household duties between them, but Ms. A.K. always looked up to her cousin as her intellectual and social leader. The cousin made the major decisions for them. She decided where they should live, where they would dine, where they should vacation, and all other matters. Ms. A.K. entered easily into this relationship, and so they lived comfortably together for several decades.

After the initial diagnostic interviews were completed, it was clear that Ms. A.K. was suffering from a painful rupture of the transference bond she had formed with her companion as a result of the sudden alteration in their functions: Ms. A.K. no longer could view her companion as her leader; in effect, she had lost the compass that had steered her life since she was a young woman. The therapeutic diagnosis was that she should enter into psychoanalytic psychotherapy.

A segment of the initial phase of her psychotherapy is as follows:

Ms. A.K.: I didn't understand what you were saying last time. You said that my cousin and I were not just friends, but that I experienced her often—or all the time—as my caretaker. I believe that's the word you used. In other words, she was always my leader and I her follower. Well, I suppose that is true, but you left out the fact that she is strong-willed and stubborn and I've had difficulties in living with her because of that. And she hurt my feelings often, I must tell you. She often does *not* listen to me or respect my wishes. Now that she is ill, she is so demanding; I'm running all day to fulfill her demands. She is not very grateful for all my work on her behalf. (*cries*) She said the other day, "You always dawdle, you've always dawdled. You've been dawdling since you were a youngster." That really hurt my feelings. I'm nothing to her. After all these years, I'm still nothing to her. (*cries*)

Therapist: Once again you're experiencing her in that special way of which we spoke—she as master, you as serf. When you get into that state, you're immobilized, very much the way you were as a youngster at home.

Transference is the great enemy of empathy. As soon as the patient entered into her transferential world, she as the slave and her companion as the plantation owner, she could not empathize with the sick, tired woman her cousin had become.

As a roundup of these segments was continued to demonstrate the "what" of her dilemma, the phenomenological complex that constituted her difficulty (phase 1 of psychotherapy), the therapist could turn to the genetic underpinnings of her problem (phase 2 of psychotherapy), and then finally to the working-through phase. Her present dilemma was interpreted as the self-object transference onto her cousin of the idealized features of her past caretakers. This is a segment from this phase.

Therapist: From what we now know of your background, it seems that you experience your cousin as a representation of your mother, that is, you pedestalize her so that her comments become commands that have to be obeyed. Further, it seems that what she says is law, to be accepted, and that her decisions are final. Finally, it seems clear that what she says are never opinions. If she says you are inadequate, you *are* inadequate. She is without question the purveyor of worth and the purveyor of life.

Ms. A.K.: Where am I to go? My cousin is everything to me. I suppose I do pedestalize her because . . . I know that you'll say that it's my experience of her, not that she is *actually* my boss.

With consistent interpretations of her structuring of her relationship with her cousin along transference lines, this patient did achieve considerable freedom from the unconscious wishes to manufacture a self-object. She was able to be a better friend and source of support throughout her lifelong companion's dying period.

One of the more important overviews for psychotherapists of the elderly to maintain is to be modest in the goals for the treatment, with a *gram* of salt. An outcome that was helpful to this patient, Ms. A.K. (and not so incidentally to her companion), was that she diminish her proclivity to enter into a transference relationship in so many of her interpersonal interactions. This may not be the most desirable outcome in an "ordinary" case of intensive psychotherapy, but in a person with a lifelong set of adaptations and defense transferences, a diminution of her maladaptive transferences is a desirable goal. The therapist's goals must take into account these variables so that when the patient demonstrates sufficient change to have an impact on his or her life, this is to be considered good progress.

Ms. A.K.: I believe it, I believe it. I actually did not fall apart when my cousin became unduly critical last evening. I believe even an antique piece like myself can change. Of course she doesn't stop. When I didn't respond, she went on and on, and on, and on. And then. . . .

The patient continued to be seen for approximately one year after her companion died. She was in good equilibrium. The therapist still sees her several times a year and talks to her several more times a year.

In the following chapter, the use of psychoanalysis for some elderly patients is discussed.

7

Psychoanalysis in the Elderly

Psychoanalysis is the therapy of choice for patients who suffer with a pervasive disturbance of character or self of such proportions that in many areas—in their involvement in work, in their interactions with other people—there are minimal gratifications or even despair. On the other hand, people suffering with a widespread self-disturbance are often excellent achievers in intellectual or artistic pursuits or in business, but without gratification. Often these patients have attempted to obtain relief from their despair through other forms of psychotherapy, which have not been helpful. The specific indication for psychoanalysis, apart from the finding that the person has a chronic self-deficit, is that such people require a reliving and reexamining of the earliest self/selfobject relations in the repeated reliving of the archaic self/selfobject encounters in the transference analysis in order to diminish the impact of their early trauma on their present lives.

And what of psychoanalysis in the elderly (Freud, 1912a, 1913, 1914; Greenson, 1967)? While Freud was in general pessimistic about it, some elderly patients can and should be treated with psychoanalysis and psycho-analytic therapy. It is true that these techniques require a great deal from both patients and practitioners. Freud himself documented the requirements in his papers on technique and on Dora (Freud, 1912a, 1912b, 1905): Pa-tients, he said, must be capable of entering into an in-vestigation of their distress and, further, they must be capable of forming a transference that they will ulti-mately be able to study, resolve, and finally discard. For Freud, as for all practitioners of analysis, the duration of the analysis was reflective of the extent of the work necessary to uncover the pathogenic repressions that maintain the transference neurosis, the central stage of the analysis. These remarks imply that the patient, in order to enter into psychoanalysis, must be capable of forming a bond of trust, of being self-observing (i.e., capable of introspection and empathy), and must have a host of other ancillary variables, such as adequate in-telligence.

What was Freud's objection to the elderly as analytic subjects? As he said (Freud, 1924), "Near and above the fifties, the elasticity of the mental processes on which the treatment depends is as a rule lacking—old people are no longer educable, and on the other hand, the mass of material to be dealt with would prolong the duration of the treatment indefinitely." Earlier he had stated (Freud, 1898), "Psychoanalysis loses its effectiveness after the patient is too advanced in years."

While the basic criteria (the capacity for trust and for self-observing and forming a transference) remain es-sential for a patient to enter into and derive relief from an analysis, the analysis of the elderly also demands "elasticity," as Freud said, on the part of both analyst and analysand.

An analysis of an elderly patient requires a great deal from both the patient and the practitioner. From the side of the patient, there are instances in which the therapist is required to "be" a selfobject, as in a supportive relationship. The patient may be responding to the loss of a dear friend and is entitled to a haven in which to discharge the grief. The patient may be ill or be lacking in energy, thus requiring the analyst to minimize the work of analysis during these times. The patient may have a hearing problem that is more apparent on some days than on others and so needs adjustments on the part of the analyst. The patient's mental capacities may be slower on some days than on others, and once again, empathic tuning-in is important in reminding the analyst to be flexible—there are days when the sessions are shorter and the "work" less strenuous.

From the side of the analyst, there are several unique concerns in working with elderly patients. In the elderly, the therapist's transferences become perhaps more visible than in any other treatment population. Who among us does not have some unresolved business with our parental selfobjects? The therapist's transferences, since they represent those idiosyncratic fixations that have not been able to be sufficiently mastered, run the gamut of unresolved selfobject needs, pregenital and oedipal strivings, and adolescent strivings for firming of one's self-cohesion, all directed momentarily by displacement and projection onto the patient. All of a sudden the therapist will feel or be disappointed in a patient or experience anxiety when the patient is vituperative or be unable to agree with the patient on termination. For a time, the therapist's empathic resources will be on strike. Is resolution of an analysis—especially an analysis with an elderly patient—reflective of a resolution in the therapist's transferences, as well as the patient's transference resolution? Does each therapy serve as yet another instance in which the therapist works through unresolved longings or unresolved transference disappointment and hatred?

In summary, to this point, psychoanalysis is the treatment of choice for those elderly patients with a self or character disorder; however, it must be approached by both analyst and analysand with care and caution. It requires of the analyst that the analyst maintain a vigilant empathic stance toward the minute-to-minute psychological and somatic capacities and needs of the patient. It requires a minute-to-minute surveillance on the analyst's part of his/her transference reactivity to the patient.

CASE HISTORY OF AN ANALYSIS*

Ms. C.H., a 75-year-old widow, entered analysis seeking relief for her painful state of depression manifested in lifelong attitudes of bitterness and futility. One of her major complaints was her inability to pursue her writing career.

In her initial interview, she related that she had become "bitter and blue" over the past several years. Her

---

*See Chapter 4, pages 76–80, for initial description of Ms. C.H.

husband had died five years previously, and while his death was saddening, it was expected. He had been ill with chronic congestive failure for several years and had been in and out of hospitals. One year after his death, she removed herself from her writing life and her social and family life and "went into a cocoon," reading and watching television. Her regression became so profound over the past 12 months that there were days when she did not get out of bed. She was referred for psychiatric treatment when a trial of antidepressants prescribed by her internist, whom she finally consulted, failed to give her relief for her painful anergia and loneliness. In the past year, her mood had become more saddened and suicidal thoughts began to emerge. Occasionally, angry thoughts directed at her husband would intrude into her psyche and elicit feelings of shame.

In the early interviews, she began, slowly at first, to express the well of affects that were evoked by her husband's death. The crying in which she now engaged—soft sobbing—became a prominent part of the next several sessions, alternating with long periods of silence. She then began to tell of the long period before his death when she had to function as his caretaker while he slowly died. It was a difficult time; he permitted no one else to keep him company or serve him. She was unprepared for these caregiving tasks since she had been used to having servants perform these functions. Often her thoughts during his final days were of slipping away or of fantasizing his funeral, thoughts that left her with considerable shame.

After several weeks of expressing her previously pent-up grief and rage, she reported that her symptoms had considerably diminished. She was walking with more vigor, her former sleep patterns were reestablished, and she began talking about the possibility of visiting her children. The supportive therapy had been effective.

Shortly after the report of the lifting of her depression, the patient—perhaps in response to the impending separation from the therapist as she became symptom-free—began to relate the sad history of her marriage and her previous life. She reported a lifelong self pattern of being unable to form relationships adequate to provide emotional nurturance. It became clear that these resistances had never allowed her to engage in a fruitful life; psychotherapy was long overdue. Ms. C.H. agreed to start an analysis when she was presented with the prescription for her cure.

The first period of her analysis represented her attempts to defend against entering into a therapeutic transference. She was preoccupied with her doubts as to the value of the analysis, not because she felt she was too old for it, but because she felt she could not change. In session after session, she insisted that the analyst could not be of service to her and that she did not have sufficient life force to undergo an analysis. The analyst's initial attempts at sharing with her her inner experience were met with rebuffs. Clearly, she rejected the interest in empathizing with her perceived sense of futility and emptiness. However, after what seemed an interminable period, she began to be less rejecting of the analyst's empathic reflections of her perceived inner state and acknowledged the accuracy of the clarifications and simple elaborations. In going over the tapes of this phase, the analyst was able to recapture the experience of working very hard and of a sad anticipation of failure. The patient seemed to be so insistent that the analysis would not benefit her. There were many instances in this phase of analysis in which the analyst noted an unfamiliar feeling of futility. Further, the analyst found himself experiencing, during this phase, many instances of self-criticism for making an inaccurate therapeutic diagnosis, extending to the notion that the patient after all was an aging woman who should not be subjected to the rigors of an analysis.

The next phase of her psychoanalysis consisted of the development of a selfobject transference in which she felt soothed and supported by the empathic interpretations and acknowledged that she valued the therapy. Then she began timidly to approach her stifled interest in her writing career, announcing one day that an editor friend had invited her to submit a short story to a magazine with which he was associated. In subsequent sessions, she associated her reemerging creative interests with the therapist's reactions. Would there be any measure of criticism in his reactions to her writing?

When her story was accepted for publication, she became anxious and withdrawn. Her associations focused on her recollections of an overprotective childhood during which her mother stressed conformity to the dress and manners of her well-to-do country-club culture. She knew at a young age that she was to serve as a "decoration" for her mother. She was going to be trained and groomed only to secure a good marriage. She had to keep secret her passion for literature and creative writing. Two older sisters were shadowy figures to her from whom she derived little comfort. Her father, a "spoiled" and withdrawn man, had little contact with his children when they were young and spent most of his time pursuing various hobbies, such as coin collecting. However, as Ms. C.H. became an adolescent, he displayed interest (when out of the mother's presence) in the books she was reading. She began showing him her poetry, which he admired. From their early interactions, she had quickly learned of her mother's selective indifference to her literary interests. For example, when she would come home from school with a story or exercise that was highly praised, her mother would change the subject and make comments about her hair or dress being messy.

In her psychoanalysis, the material shifted from anxiety about whether or not the therapist would read the story once it was published to angry accusations that he was pushing her into this activity. She accused the therapist of being interested "only" in pushing her into activity. "Why couldn't he let her alone?" She accused him of being overprotective. He wouldn't let her "goof off" and go on vacations. The analytic rules regarding the frequency of visits and free associating felt like "ropes" around her neck. This line of material continued with many variations but always involved the same theme of the therapist as tyrant—critical of her wishes to "play" and unsympathetic to her weaknesses. A segment from a taped session at that period in her analysis is as follows:

Ms. C.H.: On the whole, O.K. yesterday, the piece was going well; the words came easy. I left the office, came home to polish some more. All of a sudden—bang! I was on the couch sobbing! Oh my! I suddenly felt so lonely! After a while, I picked up the phone and went berserk, calling up everyone under the sun. What happened to me? I hate this life! I hate it! Hate it! Hate it! I have no intention of going through life like this! Empty, empty, empty! No more. I'm leaving this life! I can't stand these spells of nothingness.

I'm telling you, I can't stand it! Where are you when I need you? It's late at night; I'm all alone. You're going to be there sooner or later, but where are you when I'm all alone? (*cries*) It's always that way. Oh my! I quit! (*silence*) You made me what I am today, I hope you're satisfied—that's the old song. You pushed me into this. Why didn't you leave well enough alone? What good is it to write if loneliness is at the other end of the tunnel? Do you know what it's like to be so alone? You're never alone. You're with your family or your friends, I suppose. Do you ever think of your patient in her empty little cave? You know what I go through. Couldn't you check up on me once in a while? A little telephone call—would that break you? Ah, what's the use of talking? You're just going to "understand" and "understand" and "understand." (*long silence*)

Therapist: You must have experienced that old sensation last night that when you are creating no one is with you, in fact, you're being rejected. You must be experiencing the feeling that I, too, do not support your work.

Ms. C.H.: Well, what do I have to do to show you that I need you to care? You know I'm so panicked when I'm working that sooner or later I'm going to run or drink or commit an act of sabotage. It's always been that way. Oh God, when will I be able to write without fear? I'm telling you, this is my last venture. If this time I start running, it's the last time I try. I'm sick of the scene—prizes followed by panic. And she's always there—that witch—screaming in my ears: "I told you so, I told you so, I told you so." She always would say, "What's wrong with getting married and providing a good home? Be like me." The stupid ninny.

Yeah, well I know you're not like she is. You know how long I've been at this old saw? I remember coming home from school—over a million years ago—with a good report card. I'd say, "Hey, mother look-a-here"! Suddenly she'd grab a brush and start brushing my hair! She never read my stories. She'd always change the subject when I talked to her about anything besides clothes or boys. (*cries*)

The therapist's inner responses to the patient's accusations were, to begin with, an unfamiliar feeling of weakness. She seemed so firm in her convictions of being abused. The next response was a wish immediately to make clear her transference rather than to allow the transference to unfold itself without curtailing the full measure of her many decades of outrage at being pushed into activities she found objectionable. In effect, this amounted to a wish to be recognized immediately as an important and benevolent helper rather than to allow the transference of hatred to continue, with its implication of the threat of abandonment.

When the story was published, her rages at the therapist for being responsible for the "exposure" rose to a peak of animus. With the continuing exposure of the hated and feared negative aspects of her mother, she began tentatively to talk of her new ideas and to invite the therapist to look at them. This introduced the next phase of analysis, which consisted of a mixture of relating to the analyst in a "show and tell" manner regarding her artistic activities and threatening to quit the analysis and "goof off." In each instance in which the patient threatened to quit the analysis, the therapist became familiar with the experience of a self state of weakness and sadness. At times, this was displayed in a period of inhibition—not therapeutic abstinence—to which the patient would respond by inquiring: "Are you still there?" At other times, the analyst became aware of an archaic experience of disappointment at not having the benefits of her analysis and her analyst being appropriately recognized by the patient. However, basically the analysis was now one in which she experienced the sessions and her relationship with the therapist as an integral part of her life. Symptomatically, her complaints of emptiness and diminished self-esteem were no longer prominent, nor was her previously pervasive hypochondriasis. This phase of equilibrium was, of course, interrupted many times by a foray into her previous accusations of how the therapist had stifled her independence, coddled her, and was impervious to her wishes to retire from life. The clarifications resulted each time in more childhood memories of the disappointing events with her unempathic parents, especially the repetitious insistence on her being "just another debutante for sale in the market."

In the fourth year of her analysis, she decided to go to the Orient on an art tour. This decision came after she had worked through her experience of the therapist as being against her "freedom." Shortly after her departure, he received a call from one of her relatives stating that Ms. C.H. had had a bad fall on the trip, had fractured her ankle, and was returning home. The therapist visited her both in the hospital and at her home and resumed the analytic work as she was recovering.

At this point, she resumed her defense transference to significant proportions. Also, for the first time, material related to her advancing age, mortality, eventual death, and eventual separation from the therapist emerged.

Something now changed in the therapist's responses. At this phase of her analytic work, her complaint resulted in his more leisurely confrontation of her ongoing wish to come under his thumb in an attempt to stop her creative work. The important change in the therapist was a lessening of the inner reactions of weakness or fear to her separation threats. Suddenly, it seemed that her complaints and accusations could be listened to without interruption or that her revelation of dismay could be carried on into the following session without being "resolved" in the session in which it started.

What had occurred to effect the change in the therapist's inner reactions? One variable that could be isolated was the familiarity and, therefore, desensitization, of hearing the patient's common complaints of—and underlying wishes for—imposed tyranny. It was also clear that the analyst had, without attempting to, isolated those instances in which he had had an intense reaction—of weakness, sadness, rage at not being appreciated—and had been associating to these experiences, albeit not in a systemic manner. It was clear that the associations revealed the reexperiencing of a familiar self/selfobject interaction centering on the lack of recognition and futile attemps to call forth responses. As the patient in her working-through activities railed at the analyst who was curtailing her freedom, he was working through his revived experiences of not being sufficiently appreciated. While the patient was exploding at the analyst for taking advangage of his power over her, his revived inner experiences were that of a youngster, once again not sufficiently appreciated for his good deeds. The side-by-side working through was sufficiently diminished at the end of the analysis so that the analyst could hear her termination wishes as signs of progress rather than as repeated comments on his lack of interest.

An examination of the taped material from this analysis revealed that the analyst was much more reactive to the material than he had been in other analyses, as seen by the number of confrontations and interpretations given, especially during periods of negatively tinged material as, for example, in the instances of the defense transference.

Over time, these inner reactions constituting the transference were isolated and studied sufficiently to diminish these intrusive experiences and the behaviors that they fueled. However, during the termination phase of the analysis, the patient's regression into a revival of her complaints at being stifled and unloved provoked a feeling of uneasiness in the analyst.

Discussion

As previously indicated, psychoanalysis is the therapy of choice for those patients who suffer with a self-disturbance—a character disorder—in which so much of their self is disrupted that they cannot engage in either work or play with the appropriate joy or contentment and without shame or fear.

Are the indications for analysis in the elderly any different? Psychoanalysis is the therapy of choice when the self is so riddled with deficits that ordinary activities cannot be performed without a variety of painful experiences related to an enfeebled self: doubting, denying, and ineptitude. Those who benefit from analysis clearly cannot be in a state of crisis—fragmentation. In those cases where sector or psychoanalytic therapy seems the therapy of choice, the therapist has concluded that the patient's overall self-cohesiveness, apart from the problem area, is not afflicted and that the therapist and the patient can proceed to isolate the sector for study and clarification. The patient requires the therapist to be an ally in psychoanalytic therapy, thus precluding any detailed scrutiny of the patient's attitudes toward the therapist.

The essentials of the cure in analysis are based on the reliving and reexamining of the early pathogenic traumas now transferred onto the analyst and the analyst/analysand relationship. Ultimately, these toxic transferences will be revealed and deenergized (the neutralizing of the defense transference) so that the patient can accept the analyst and the ministrations of acceptance and affirming in order to internalize the analyst's selfobject functions and to experience self-worth and self-admiring, one of the end points of an analysis designed to promote the growth of the self. Another goal of an analysis is to understand in depth the influences that the past has had on the present, especially in determining the ability to derive succor and leadership from the human encounter.

For any analysis to proceed, the requirements of the analysand are that he or she cannot be in a state of fragmentation, since the cognitive functions must be intact for the work of free association to proceed. The patient must have a tested capacity for introspection and empathy and be able to experience trust in the analyst.

As for the selection of analysis as the therapy of choice for the elderly, the indications are the same for any person who presents for relief of an enfeebled self, a self that does not work, a self that cannot provide the requisite gratification to ensure equilibrium in any environment. There is not enough assertiveness to seek out human sources of calming or admiration or there is so much resistance to the impact of warmth that loneliness continues.

What of the requirements for the elderly as patients to engage in analysis? Apart from the usual requirements of trust, the capacity for alliance formation, and the prediction that there will not be interminability (i.e., the self is not mired in adhesive selfobject fixations and, therefore, incapable of change), the requirements for entering into and continuing in analysis for the elderly also include (1) the continued integrity of their selves, especially during the times of anxiety and regression aroused in the analysis; and (2) a reasonably good physiological status so that they can continue in analysis for several sessions per week.

From the analyst's point of view, the requirements are that (1) an empathic diagnosis be made in each session of the patient's capacity to accept interpretations, confrontations, and silence; (2) the analyst needs to function as an selfobject when indicated, for example, during times of illness or mourning; and (3) the analyst's own transferences toward the elderly, including fears of deterioration, death, and uneasiness, must be at an optimum, and when there is an intrusion of transference on the analyst's functioning, that the necessary self-analytic work will be performed.

Another aspect of analysis for the elderly is its termination. There are those elderly patients who require lifelong contact after the analysis. For some, the contact is a phone call every few months, while for others, a few informal sessions a year are sufficient. Postanalytic patients must also be aware that if an important event occurs, the analyst will be available for discussions and to help with decision making.

GOALS IN PSYCHOANALYSIS FOR THE ELDERLY

As indicated, psychoanalysis is the psychotherapy of choice for those selves so riddled with deficits that ordinary activities cannot be performed without pain—the pain of an enfeebled self caught up in pervasive doubting or demeaning or ineptitude. Those patients of any age who require analysis have selves that do not "work," that is, they cannot provide the requisite gratifications to maintain self-cohesion regardless of the human environment. Patients with these incomplete selves are not patients in a state of crisis or fragmentation. Psychoanalysis is the therapy for those whose selves are *not* in crisis or distress in reaction to a particular surround; it is their intrapsychic perceptions and reactions that cause their distress. Further, their entire selves cannot be in a fragmented state for the work of analysis to proceed, thus precluding its use for any patient in a state of crisis as a result of pursuing psychoanalysis as the therapy of choice.

The goals for any analysis are as follows:

Psychoanalysis has as its goal that the self will be transformed: significantly more assertiveness will be manifest; there will be selfobjects sought after for human succor in time of need; and there will be more in the way of ideals experienced, through which the self will be led to greater achievements. The entire activities of the self will be devoted in part to the pursuit of a joyous existence. (Muslin & Val, 1987, p. 161)

What should be added to the specific goals for the elderly self should be to answer the question: who requires analysis? In work with the elderly, the factors of time and energy impose, on both analyst and analysand, limitations on the extent of the working-through process. In analysis with most adults, we are used to pursuing freely, without restraint, any instance in which the archaic defense transferences, for example, may continue to be reenacted. In the elderly, our awareness of the finitude of their active lives or their lives without massive infirmity urges us to make judgments about terminating analysis we need not make, nor should we make, in analysis with younger patients. Making a judgment about termination in this manner constitutes an exception to the ordinary method of doing psychoanalysis. However, it is an important exception, ensuring that these patients will be enabled to utilize the benefits of a transference analysis. The analyst is called on in the psychoanalysis of the elderly to make decisions that are not ordinarily within the province of a "hands-off" psychoanalyst. However, as with all of the psychotherapies performed with the elderly, flexibility informed by the observations of empathy is the crucial therapeutic guide.

Thus, in some patients, the diagnosis that a termination can be effected comes about when many areas of the self are functioning better—the capacity for bonding, for example, and for insight into one's resistances to forming human bonds is enhanced. Still, in some areas of their interpersonal world, with their children or with a friend, an archaic self/selfobject interaction may continue to be reenacted. Or in a somewhat similar fashion, a patient's overall functioning has been considerably improved, but the patient continues to resist performing or resuming activities that would ensure the patient's self-esteem, such as returning to work after the death of a spouse or taking up a hobby or activity that afforded them pleasure in the past. In each of these instances, the analyst should not object if the patient wishes to consider termination even if he or she has not "completely" worked through all the situations in which the archaic self/selfobject fixations continue to be manifest.

With these exceptions, psychoanalysis should continue to be recommended in the elderly without reluctance.

We will now turn to the therapist's inner world as it affects—negatively and positively—the psychotherapy of the elderly.

8

The Inner World
of the Therapist
of the Elderly

Psychotherapy cannot proceed without the psychotherapist's reactions being at an optimum, especially with regard to the therapist's transferences and countertransferences. As previously stated (Muslin & Clarke, 1988), "Psychoanalysis and psychoanalytic therapy requires a great deal from its patients and its practitioners" (p. 295). Perhaps the greatest demand on therapists is to be ever-mindful of their inner reactions to the patient and to the patient's material. These inner reactions include the therapist's own transference reactions and reactions to the patient's transference onto the therapist, the so-called countertransference reactions. While much interest has been shown in therapists' reactions to psychotherapy patients in general, the inner reactions of the therapist of the elderly have received little attention (Grotjahn, 1955; Hiatt, 1972; Kaufman, 1940; Meerloo, 1951; Muslin & Clarke, 1988).

The transferences of the therapist refer to those self-reactions in which the therapist, with minimal overt stimuli from the patient, experiences reactions that clearly represent displacements onto the patient from the therapist's internal gallery of selfobjects and objects. In the midst of a transference reaction, the patient's material can only be seen from *this* perspective and empathy is effectively stifled; transference is, after all, the great antagonist to empathy. The therapist's transferences are a virtually unexplored area in the psychotherapy theory of cure. However, they are important ingredients to be continually observed so as not to interfere, or to be of minimal interference, with the empathic tasks required of the therapist. An unobserved transference reaction will interfere in each phase of psychotherapy, from the diagnostic phase to the termination of the treatment.

The transference reactions of therapists have not been sufficiently examined throughout the course of a psychotherapy so as to be able to delineate these reactions as we can for a patient going through transference. In whatever way therapists become aware of their transference reactions in a particular case, those reactions that reflect their unfulfilled longings and/or sensitivities and fears are important to trace to their roots in the therapist's inner world. To repeat, each unobserved—and, therefore, undiagnosed—transference reaction affects the empathic work and the entire therapy from diagnosis to termination.

The therapist's countertransference reactions represent one aspect of the total transference reactions to the patient. They call attention to the transference reactions of the therapist as evoked by the patient's transference reactions onto the therapist. In such situations, the patient's behaviors are evocative of some type of unspecified reaction and thus the therapist's responses are a result of the evocative stimulus—the patient's transferences—and the therapist's specific intrapsychic responses. Therapists vary widely in their capacity to experience their patients' transference reactions while continuing to maintain their empathic stance, again indicating that element of the therapists' idiosyncratic transferences that is involved in each clinical situation. The clinical literature describes many instances in which the so-called countertransference reactions went undetected until they were revealed through some type of action that was unhelpful to the progress of treatment. Other instances are reported in the literature in which the countertransference reactions ultimately led to the clarification of the patient's transference reactions (Kohut, 1971; Racker, 1957; Tower, 1956).

In some psychotherapy situations, the therapist's inner world may become filled with "nontransferential" love or hate or ambivalent strivings toward a particular patient. These reactions arise in relationships in which the transference phenomenon—as in all relationships—plays a minor role. The therapist experiences the patient as an attractive or an outrageous person, a "civilian" who offers the possibility for a love affair or a hostile encounter. In each case of these nontransferential "civilian" reactions, the therapists are immersed in their wishes to engage their patients in a positive or negative manner as one does a prospective companion or with someone in a familiar relationship, even a negative one. And just as with a prospective companion, there may be hidden transference longings for an archaic selfobject, as well as a source of peer gratification (mature selfobject).

Every psychotherapeutic relationship involves instances in which the therapist's reactions are important to evaluate—the transference and nontransference reactions. These transference reactions run the gamut of unresolved selfobject needs, pregenital and oedipal strivings to adolescent strivings for firming of one's self-cohesion, all directed by displacement and projection onto the patient. Similarly, the patient may suddenly be viewed as an ordinary person who either is an admirable person or is unapproachable or angering, thus denying the status of the patient and the role of the therapist. In all these instances, therapists find themselves experiencing reactions apart from their diagnostic or therapeutic mission: the therapist is angry at an "ungrateful" patient; the therapist is eager to see a particular patient; the therapist is saddened or anxious when the patient is angered; the therapist cannot agree with the patient on a date for termination or cannot agree that the patient is ready for termination. In all these instances and for varying periods, the therapist's empathic resources are on strike.

The following vignettes from the writings of psychotherapy authors illustrate the ubiquity and complexity of the self-intrusions into the therapist's psychotherapeutic mission.*

Example 1 (from Freud)

Persuasive evidence of a transference is contained in the meeting between Freud and Dora when Dora

*These examples are taken from Muslin & Val (1987)

came to see Freud fifteen months after the treatment was over. He says that she came to ask for help, but "one glance at her face, however, was enough to tell me that she was not in earnest over her request" (Freud, 1905, pp. 120-121). How he possibly could have told this from one glance at her face remains a mystery, and, indeed, the evidence he subsequently gives to indicate that she was not in earnest is unconvincing.

She said that she had come for help with her right-sided facial neuralgia, and when he asked how long it had been going on, she said, "two weeks." Freud said that he couldn't help smiling, and he was able to show her that two weeks before she had read some news about him in the newspaper. Strachey tells us that this was no doubt news of Freud's appointment to a professorship (p. 122).

But how do we know what this news meant to her? Even though Freud says he did not know what she wanted, he offers the explanation that her facial neuralgia was a self-punishment, remorse for having given Herr K. a box on the ear and at having transferred her feelings of revenge to him. Despite the fact that Dora had come on her own, rather than, as at first, at her father's bidding, Freud says nothing about the possibility of her positive attachment to him nor does he recognize any genuine desire for help. It may be that his own positive transference led him to reject the implicit wish in her seeking him out—i.e., to renew their relationship. In any event, Freud apparently terminated the interview quickly and never saw her again. (Muslin and Gill, 1978)

Example 2 (from Gitelson, 1952)

At the beginning of an hour in an ongoing analysis, a young male patient commented to me that I looked tired. I myself was not aware of fatigue. Towards the end of the hour, which he had spent talking about his university activities, he requested a change in the time of his appointment two weeks hence, when he was scheduled to present a paper in a seminar. I responded that I would see what I could do about changing the time. He then retracted his request, giving as his reason that it would inconvenience me. I told him, however, that the request seemed valid and that I would see what change I could make in his appointment. He left my office looking preoccupied.

The next day he brought the following dream: He has an engagement with his mother but it seems to be incidental to a date which he has later with his mistress. He acts as if he were indifferent to his mother and is hurried in disposing of the business with her.

The patient then spoke of how upset he felt after the previous hour. I told him that I had noticed it. Then he spoke about not writing home and about his childhood feeling that he was incidental to his mother's career interests. His further comments made it clear that he now ignored the existence of his parents, as he had himself felt ignored. Then he referred to my "insistence" on rearranging my program for him, *even after he felt that he had detected some hesitancy on my part.*

At this point something occurred to me which I had

until then forgotten: On the morning of the day of my patient's request, I had arrived earlier than usual at the hospital for the purpose of discussing cases with the residents. None of them were around and none appeared until I was about to leave with only a limited time in which to reach my office. They had been disappointed because I could not stay on to work with them. I myself had been irked by their lateness and had commented on it. But the matter had apparently slipped my mind.

I shall not go into the personal ramifications of this episode. But it was clear to me that I had displaced my reaction in the hospital situation to him. I did the only thing I felt I could do: I brought the episode into the open and admitted the irritation, which I recognized I had produced, without awareness, against him. It developed, however, that what had affected him most was that he had correctly observed my compensatory attitude. This had impressed him as a concern for something in myself rather than for him. That this was more important than my apparent annoyance with him was shown when he told me that his mother had often said that she was doing something for his good when the fact was that it was something in which she had a personal stake. (Gitelson, 1952)

Example 3 (from Tower, 1956)

One beautiful spring day I walked out of my office, twenty minutes before this patient's hours, with my appointment book lying open on my desk. I had a delicious luncheon, alone, which I enjoyed more than usual, and strolled back to the office, in time for my next appointment, only to be informed that my patient had been there and had left extremely angry. It was obvious that I had forgotten her appointment, unconsciously and purposely, and it suddenly came over me that I was absolutely fed up with her abuse to the point of nonendurance. At this point, I began to be angry at my patient, and between this time and the next time she came in, I was in a substantial rage against her. Part of this rage I related to guilt and part to some anxiety about how I would handle the next treatment interview, which I expected would surpass all previous abuse, and I was not aware of the fact that I was no longer going to be able to tolerate this abuse. I fantasied (which of course was a hope) that my patient would terminate her treatment with me.

At her next appointment, she glared at me and said, in an accusatory manner, "Where were you yesterday?" I said only, "I'm sorry, I forgot." She started to attack me, saying she knew I had been there shortly before, and went on with her customary vituperation. I made no comment, for the most part feeling it was better that I say nothing. This went on for five or ten minutes and abruptly she stopped. There was a dead silence and all of a sudden she started to laugh, saying, "Well, you know, Dr. Tower, really I can't say that I blame you." This was absolutely the first break in this obstinate resistance. Following this episode, the patient was much more cooperative and after one or two short recurrences of the abusiveness, probably to test me, the defense disappeared entirely, and she shortly went into analysis at deep transference levels. At first glance, this seems so unimportant an episode that it hardly warrants description. One would say I was irritated with the patient and missed her hour because of aggression, which of course was true. But the real countertransference problem was not that. Actually, my acting-out behavior was reality-based and brought a resolution to the countertransference problem, which was that I had been patient with her too long. This tendency in myself I could trace in detail from certain influences on me in my earliest childhood. I had gotten into difficulties from this tendency from time to time during my development. I understood this in part, and yet it was not sufficiently resolved in my personality. This prolonged abusive resistance need not have lasted so long had I been freer to be more aggressive in the face of it. The manner in which I repressed my aggression and allowed it to accumulate to a point where I was forced to act it out was not an entirely desirable therapeutic procedure. Thus, a theoretically good therapeutic attitude, namely, that of infinite patience and effort to understand a very troubled patient, was actually in this situation a negative countertransference structure, virtually a short-lived countertransference neurosis, which undoubtedly wasted quite a bit of the patient's time, and but for my sudden resolution of it through acting out, might well have gone on for a considerably longer time. I gave this little episode a good deal of thought in subsequent years, and eventually came to understand more of its true significance. (Tower, 1956)

Example 4 (from Kohut, 1971)

As I gradually began to realize, the analysand assigned to me a specific role within the framework of the world view of a very young child. During this phase of the analysis the patient had begun to remobilize an archaic, intensely cathected image of the self which had heretofore been kept in insecure repression. Concomitant with the remobilization of the grandiose self, on which she had remained fixated, there also arose the renewed need for an archaic object (a precursor of psychological structure) that would be nothing more than the embodiment of a psychological function which the patient's psyche could not yet perform for itself: to respond empathically to her narcissistic display and to provide her with narcissistic sustenance through approval, mirroring, and echoing.

Due to the fact that I was at that time not sufficiently alert to the pitfalls of such transference demands, many of my interventions interfered with the work of structure formation. But I know that the obstacles that stood in the way of my understanding lay not only in the cognitive area; and I can affirm, without transgressing the rules of decorum and without indulging in the kind of immodest self-revelation which ultimately hides mores than it admits, that there were specific hindrances in my own personality which stood in the way. There was a residual insistence, related to deep and old fixation points, on seeing myself in the narcissistic center of the state; and, although I had of course for a long time struggled with the relevant childhood delusions and thought that I had, on the whole, achieved dominance over them, I was temporarily unable to cope with the cognitive task posed by the confrontation with the reactivated grandiose self of my patient. Thus I refused to entertain the possibility that I was not an object for the patient, not an amalgam with the patient's childhood loves and hatreds, but only, as I reluctantly came to see, an impersonal function, without significance except insofar as it related to the kingdom of her own remobilized narcissistic grandeur and exhibitionism.

For a long time I insisted, therefore, that the patient's reproaches related to specific transference fantasies and wishes on the oedipal level—but I could make no headway in this direction. It was ultimately, I believe, the high-pitched tone of her voice which led me on the right track. I realized that it expressed an utter conviction of being right—the conviction of a very young child—which had heretofore never found expression. Whenever I did more (or less) than provide simple approval or confirmation in response to the patient's report of her own discoveries, I became for her the depressive mother who (sadistically, as the patient experienced it) deflected the narcissistic cathexes from the child upon herself, or who did not provide the needed narcissistic echo. Or I became the brother, who, as she felt, twisted her thoughts and put himself into the limelight. (Kohut, 1971)

And now to turn to the inner world of the therapist of the elderly which, as we are aware, determines or influences all phases of psychotherapy work. There are special considerations to address in therapists' reactions to their elderly patients; these reactions can be summarized by describing the transference and non-transferential reactions evoked in working with the elderly.

TRANSFERENCE REACTIONS
IN THE THERAPIST OF THE ELDERLY

The transferences evoked by the elderly patient catch every therapist in whatever unfulfilled longing or residual animus perists toward the elderly. Which of us does not harbor some unresolved business with our parental selfobjects? The residual wish for selfobject mirroring, certainly a commonplace, now transferred onto the selfobject/patient is revealed as one such transference experience of the psychotherapist. The behaviors will reflect those therapists attempting to derive applause or admiration from their "therapeutic" activities. Pleasing the patient to derive mirroring is inimical to the patient's progress in psychotherapy, which is to be based on the patient's needs recognized through empathic observations. These attempts by the therapist to derive mirroring will result in a variety of behaviors, ranging from withholding necessary confrontations and interpretations to honoring a patient's request for medications which should be denied. In those instances in which the patient has become a transferential mirroring selfobject to the unaware psychotherapist, the therapist will become aware of this only when the therapist becomes anxious or sad when the patient expresses displeasure at the lack of progress in the therapy or threatens to interrupt the treatment. These transferential reactions, of course, interfere with the empathic approach and, therefore, the investigation into the patient's resistances will not be initiated as the therapist attempts to mollify the patient, or is inhibited, or in whom psychomotor retardation (depressive reaction) results from the threatened loss. In those instances in which the patient has become a fantasied idealized parent selfobject, the therapist's behavior and attitudes reflect the process of becoming subservient to the patient-experienced-as-guru. Suddenly, the therapist is not investigating or confronting or seeking meanings in the patient's material, but is listening in a respectful or subservient manner and mentally taking notes while the "mentor" is speaking.

The experiences that the therapist has in these instances will reveal the phenomenon of idealization: (1) the patient's remarks are remembered throughout the day; (2) the therapist will wish to ask the patient's advice about a social or financial matter, and in some instances will actualize the wish; (3) the patient will emerge in the therapist's dreams and daydreams in roles appropriate to the patient's selfobject status as the idealized parent offering direction or calming and soothing.

A different ambience is present when the patient is invested with transferences that reflect the therapist's residual anger at his/her selfobject parents for a variety of reasons, including disappointment in their selfobject functions. The behaviors that result in these scenarios are those of the therapist's seeming inability to accept the limitations of the patient's modal age changes, whether these are evidenced in a slowed gait or slowed mentation or in the elderly patient's self-centeredness. The therapist experiences a flash of anger at the manifest limitations of the patient, indicating that the mode of reaction is now not empathic, but rather is transferential. The therapist as the relived self of infancy and childhood is again experiencing and actualizing the anger of an infant or child who is being deprived because of limitations of the parent/selfobject.

Another negative transference reaction will emerge in those instances in which the therapist's transferences onto the patient call forth behaviors in the therapist of unexpected isolation. These behaviors constitute an aspect of a reenactment of those painful experiences in the therapist's background in which the frequency of disappointment from a selfobject or inconsistency of the selfobject resulted in the therapist's defense of isolation. The therapist will be aware in these instances of a palpable *uneasiness* with the patient's material when there is an affective discharge of warmth or affection. In such situations, the therapist's responses will include the strong wish to avoid the patient and the patient's material which, in the therapist's background, was connected to the sequence of warmth by selfobjects followed by rejection from these selfobjects.

Another set of experiences and behaviors expressed by therapists at times reveals the transference experienced by some therapists of their disavowal of the fact that their patients are older people. Whether the verbal and nonverbal behaviors of these therapists are replete with sarcasms, inappropriate humor, or impatience, the inner experience—the distortion—in this category of transference is the experience of the elderly patient as a more vibrant, more vigorous version of the patient than is true of the actual patient. These transferences again reflect the negative experiences of disappointments and rejections in one's relations with one's selfobjects.

CLINICAL EXAMPLES

The following clinical vignettes highlight the therapist's transference experiences and their resolution.

Case 1. Mr. M.N.

A 74-year-old man was in a hospital intensive care unit being treated for a heart attack when he suddenly became frightened, complaining that he "could not get enough air to breathe." This anxiety attack was the only one he had in the hospital. However, in the weeks after he left the hospital, he began to have similar attacks. He would wake up suddenly in the early hours of the morning with a burst of anxiety, with the conviction that he was not getting "enough air." Becoming increasingly frightened, he would run to the refrigerator for an ice pack to place on his forehead, turn on the television set and pace around the room, attempting to calm himself. The attacks would last thirty or forty minutes. He stated that these attacks were almost identical to the heart attack except for the "squeezing" of the chest. He came to therapy for help in alleviating the attacks since he knew that they represented an anxiety state.

Mr. M.N. was dressed in a very jaunty manner, with an open-collar sports shirt and sunglasses, and looked

the picture of a robust pereson visiting in Chicago between trips to Florida or the Caribbean. He quickly informed the therapist that he had been a successful in-
dustrialist and had retired 10 months before his heart
attack. He followed this information with an overview
of his present circumstances: He had been married and
divorced three times, but had no children and he now
lived alone. He had always been a "rugged individual-
ist" since his days in college. He had left his home in
the east to go to school, and apart from occasional trips
back, he never again spent any time with his family of
origin. He had been an excellent student in high school
and also in college, where he had received an academic
scholarship. During World War II, he was a fighter pilot
in the U.S. Army Air Force. On his 21st mission, his
plane was hit and he parachuted into Germany, where
he was captured and spent several months in a prisoner-
of-war camp. Upon returning to the United States, he
dived into the hectic life of a "man determined to be a
financial success." He eventually accomplished this goal
and was able to retire with a considerable fortune. However, as he said, he never was able to share his life with
anyone, cerrtainly not with his various wives—who, he
complained, wished to "possess" him or "never would
give [him] enough space." He provided a quick resumé
of his early life in a large and poor family with a constantly overworked mother, of whom he saw little, and
an even more distant father.

The initial experiences of which the therapist became
aware in himself were of two kinds: a civilian reaction
and a transference reaction. The civilian reaction was
that the therapist found this "rugged" character an at-

tractive person whom he admired. He saw the patient's boldness and directness as refreshing, and his courage and perseverance as attractive features. He could easily empathize both with his background and with his need to stay apart from "close" human encounters.

The second reaction of which the therapist became aware in these early interviews was a transference reaction; this patient evoked in the therapist experiences of being with his own father. His father also was a large, sometimes gregarious man who in his earlier years, and during the therapist's childhood, was given to humor and to performing practical jokes. The transference reactions were of a mirroring type, the awareness of old unfulfilled wishes to derive admiration or applause from an archaic selfobject. The form in which these transferences emerged was in the experience that once again the therapist would be with someone who ultimately could not empathize with and provide him with the required affirmations. In the early phase of the therapy, when the patient would complain that the therapy did not include enough "nuts and bolts," the therapist would feel a genuine pang of fear and embarrassment, as if he had overlooked something or had not been careful enough to supply the patient with "something."

In the next phase of therapy, as the therapist identified the sector of Mr. M.N.'s self that he felt could be worked on (the need to maintain his wall against human encounters), he entered into a protracted resistance on the patient's part to working on or altering his self. In his resistance to the study of his self, the patient resorted to a variety of tactics to fend off the work of the therapy. Among these was the expert use of insult aimed at psychotherapy and its practitioners, including the therapist. He would call attention to "ivory tower people" and their preoccupation with other-worldly interests. He wondered if the therapist had ever been to a "joint" (cocktail lounge) or a ball game. Did he ever see the "real" world and "real" people? Why not let well-enough alone? What was the "big deal" in whether he overcame his inhibitions and lived differently? He was not as bad off as some. And besides, as he stated, he was not sure that the therapist wasn't just as inhibited as he was. What gave the therapist the "right" to point at him as a specially unusual person? A frequent comment during this phase was, "Come on, Doc, what's the big deal?"

The therapist's subjective reactions to these comments were varied. He would, at most times, experience with equanimity the patient's urging to dissuade him from addressing his resistance to life in a serious manner. At other times, he would experience a self-tension. His insults at the therapist's "egghead" status, in his view, did not usually cause any disruption of the therapeutic stance; however, he sometimes experienced irritation at the patient's frequently hostile comments about intellectuals in general and physicians in particular.

In going over the transcripts from this phase of the therapy, it appeared that during this time in the treatment the therapist had begun to view the patient "as a patient," that is, with a minimum of his transference reactions.

In response, perhaps, to the therapist's lack of hostility at M.N.'s comments and his offering of interpretations of his defense transference toward the therapist, Mr. M.N.'s resistances diminished. The therapy then shifted into the phase of uncovering sufficient background material to reveal the fixations, the crucial developmental information. This patient had set up a wall of defense against the egress of any dependency longings on his part, basically defending against his receptive longings toward his mother. In his view, her "bitchiness"—her constantly expressed dissatisfaction with him—was responsible for his leaving home early and never returning. There was literally no one else around to guide him or calm him. He was a "loner" from his earliest days. He learned how to rely on his quickness and his courage to get out of scrapes. He was a quick study of everything he ever had to do in life as long as it did not take a great deal of time, since he was always "impatient." Thus he never had been able to turn to reading as a source of gratification; he was too distracted. Even in college, he could never keep current with his studies, but had to finish his school work under great pressure since he could not simply sit down and accomplish it in a quiet and timely, organized manner.

He told again of his many failed attempts at letting down the "drawbridge to my heart and letting someone in." His last wife got to the point, he said, of "getting all over me. I could not stand it. I had to let her go. I told her I needed my space."

In the last phase of Mr. M.N.'s therapy, the therapist's interpretations summarized the essential theme of his past-to-present reenactment: every human encounter, in his view, was to be guarded against since it might entail "someone" picking him up temporarily and then dropping him, as he remembered his mother's behavior toward him. He was able to make substantial progress in this working-through phase—from present "safe" interactions to past "dangerous" ones—by focusing on many instances in which this dynamic was operational.

And so, therapist and patient headed for the termination phase. Mr. M.N.'s anxiety symptoms were considerably reduced so that the panic attacks were no longer a problem-in-living. His fears of the human encounter had diminished sufficiently for him to take up residence again with his most-recent former wife. Since his retirement, he had been asked by an old friend to assist him in his mail-order business. He accepted this invitation in his second year of psychotherapy, and the assistance evolved into a nearly full-time position.

After a termination date was set, the patient had a regression in which he experienced a few anxiety attacks, again marked by the conviction that he was not getting enough oxygen and was close to death. He also had a regression in his human interactions, again becoming aloof with his mate. He responded to confrontations and interpretations of the revisited defense transference and the symptoms once again diminished. And once again, the therapist confronted him with his longings and fears of the archaic selfobject now displaced onto the therapist and onto Mr. M.N.'s mate. After this transference barrier was again weakened, he could once more derive the mirroring and calming necessary to maintain his self-cohesion so that his panicky aloneness diminished.

One other piece of regressive behavior emerged in the termination phase: the patient's attacks on the therapist, which represented a reenactment (an acting out) of the patient's defending himself against the omnipotent mother. Dependency on his mother was always equated with painful rejection and so introduced the frightening state of aloneness. The situation was akin to being under the thumb of "the frightening one" and the action required was to push her away by "sticks and stones," that is, by the battle tactics of children, abusive and dismissive magical words that would defuse her power.

Throughout the therapy, the patient's reactions to the therapist included these dismissive comments, aimed at defusing the power of the therapist as a transference selfobject. They were, of course, prominent at the beginning of the therapy before the formation of the therapeutic alliance, that is, prior to the diminution of the patient's defense transference. In the midst of the combat of the defense transference—the patient struggling against the power of the magna mater who, in his view, was constantly threatening to take his life away—there was no capacity to join with the therapist in the observational work of psychotherapy. When the patient allied himself with the therapist, it represented the termination of the destructive power of the archaic selfobject. Although the therapist in psychotherapy does not center on the patient's transference in this mode of therapy, there are instances in which a focus on the patient's transference toward the therapist is necessary. These circumstances all revolve around the resistances to therapy—the temporary shutdown of or resistance to formation of the alliance. In these circumstances, the therapist is obliged to interpret the transference to the patient so that therapy can proceed.

The termination period has a built-in *da capo* effect: the patient relives the childhood self state, and with it, the childhood self/selfobject transference postures. These revisited self states perhaps reflect the resistance to change inspired by the impending separation from the past, and thus the resumption of the initial transference self state represents a wish to cling to the therapy and to the therapist without termination of the bond.

The therapist's transferences at the beginning and end of the therapy are of special significance. At the beginning of the therapy, the patient's reactions to the therapist, as noted above, at times were negatively tinged prior to the formation of the therapeutic alliance. At this stage in the therapy, the therapist's transference experiences were prominent.

The following material represents vignettes from initial interviews, which will be followed by vignettes from the termination phase of this patient's psychotherapy. These vignettes are accompanied by the therapist's recollections of his self-experiences in these sessions.

Material from an early session

Mr. M.N.: Hi there. (*silence for 30 seconds*) I had the idea after I left last time that you were not pleased with my ideas about members of your profession. Now, Doc, you got to admit, some of the people in your business are whores. Why, I went to see one of your colleagues once and I told him that part of my bill would be paid by Medicare. He looked and acted shocked and so I told him off. He was so high and mighty. You'd think I was sawdust under his feet. Lots of us weren't lucky enough to be raised with silver spoons in our mouths. I know you guys have a union and patients are patients and doctors are doctors. I know I'm carrying on too much, but I'm not that naive; I know I'm not in your league in knowledge, but dumb I'm not. It's just that you ivory-tower guys, you get to me. What would you know about a guy like me and with my background? You ever been to a joint or got loaded? Ever been in a fist fight? Because some of your comments sound like you've never been anywhere except inside a book. Sometimes I feel like telling you, "You read that in a book!"

Comments

The material arising in this session and others during this phase of defense against alliance formation and the therapy served to urge the therapist to "go away," but more significantly, it demonstrated that the patient had entered into a defense transference—the therapist was a member of an elite group and he was a plebeian. If this trend continued, there would be no mutual studying by therapist and patient. At times, the therapist's acceptance of such behaviors causes the defense transference to diminish; at other times, the therapist must interpret this transference configuration. When the defense transference becomes a major resistance, the therapist is called on to interpret: "You have begun to put me on a throne where I vent my rage on you, duplicating the exact way you experienced your relationship with your mother. It's an unconscious mechanism, an old way to get along, even though it's painful and unrewarding in the 1990's."

The therapist's experiences in no small way determine the free capacity or bound incapacity to empathize with the patient's self state and, therefore, to perform appropriately or not. If the therapist's experiences are clouded with subjective reactions of all kinds, the empathic function may become dangerously dysfunctional and the appropriate therapeutic actions will be missing from the therapy.

The therapist's internal reactions to this material were of several kinds. There was an alteration between calmness and irritation at the attempts by the patient to elicit combat. The irritation on the therapist's part amounted to a freezing of empathy while the patient entered into the experience of irritation. Suddenly, the therapist, in the patient's view, was a supercilious snob who needed to be taken off his perch. The depth of the therapist's experiences provoked the need to investigate his restimulated childhood experiences. Ancient sibling rivalries were revisited and studied so as to understand the therapist's own resistances to the work of empathically informed psychotherapy.

Clinical material from the termination

Mr. M.N.: Well, I'm pleased that we can quit as you said. It's been tough to get here these two times a week. I'm sure you'll be glad not to have to hear my complaints, although granted they are much smaller. You're a younger man, but you're not young; I imagine you've heard so much already in your lifetime. I mean I guess you want to quit at times also. I don't know what I mean today. I'm jumpy and I haven't been jumpy in quite a while. Actually, what really decides when you've had "enough" therapy? I know I'm feeling better—hell, I forgot what made me come here—but you must have some agenda, some standard, that makes you go along in an organized way. Hell, you didn't fight at all; you used to fight when I said I wanted to leave. What's the difference now? My thought is that you want to get on with other things and other people; you can't be turned on all the time. Here it is: There's a limit even though you're a professional. How much can you continue your interest—until you're jaded? You'll go your way, I'll go my way. Of course you never know. It's not precise, how far I can go. It is, after all, just an estimate as to how far I can develop into a stronger person. But that's life and you've got to go on, I suppose.

Even my wife noticed that I haven't been the same since we set the date—you know what I mean? She says I sleep so fitfully these days. I move, make sounds. I guess she's used to a cadaver. Her beauty sleep, she calls it. She puts her earphones on or earplugs in, puts that black mask over her eyes. What a sight! My appetite's off too. I'm just kind of mopey, you know what I mean? I guess it's temporary. I suppose you have these periods too? But I know you got other things and other people and I should be pleased, not grouchy and biting at you. You're a professional man. You wouldn't let other considerations influence your decision about how far to go, how much therapy a person needs and all those things. I just thought that if you were hiding some irritation toward me, it should come out. You're a person, too.

You know I never talked this way to anyone. What am I saying? It's silly, but it's funny. Those thoughts just popped into my mind. How could I think those things? That's ridiculous. But they just pop into my mind, they just pop into my mind. They're nutty thoughts, but they pop into my mind. Right now, I feel aggravated, you know, not content. I can't find a place for myself to be calm. I feel pissed off. It's got to be what's going on here right now. I've talked long enough, what do you think? I feel like I'm a prosecuting attorney but really, those thoughts just won't go away. So answer them even though they're life charges against you. Are you stopping the sessions because you think I'm O.K. the way I am or is there something else bothering you?

Comment

The emphasis in this discussion is not on the accusations of the patient—neither the content nor the intensity. The emphasis is on the reactions of the therapist which we will now highlight.

The accusations of being uncaring ("I guess you want to get on with other things . . . you got to have a limited interest in people") evoked the experience of fear on the therapist's part. These comments, coupled with the allusions to being ill ("My wife noticed I haven't been sleeping well" and "My appetite has fallen off" and "I can't find a place for myself") served to stir up familiar areas of tension. For one, deserting a person in distress is a charge that has unique implications for the therpist. Raised in an environment in which there was a significant amount of illness, the experience of not doing enough for other members of the family was a common, albeit irrational one, and one that was not mastered until much later in life. The patient's accusations were sufficient to arouse this tension surrounding caretaking so that the therapist would query himself about the appropriateness of the termination. Once he investigated these thoughts more deeply, he would listen more carefully to the patient's material as expressions of his needs of the moment or of the past. Was the termination decision appropriate? Was the patient's capacity to tolerate separation from active therapy perhaps too limited at this time? Was he bringing up material that would be present *whenever* he terminated (i.e., the revived vicissitudes of the archaic self/selfobject dyad in which he lived through self-scarring deprivation)? These queries could never be investigated if the therapist was immobilized by his own fixations.

The exhortations of the therapist's unique past now intruding on the present were that (1) each complaint is valid and must be gratified since the other person is suffering or hurting and there is no other solution but to gratify the other's expressed need—this would be the motto of the past; (2) these complaints do not have a topographical aspect—defenses against unconscious strivings—but are authentic expressions of need requiring gratification; and (3) the other's needs are much more significant than one's own needs at that moment.

These comments reflect the particular self/selfobject dyad of the past that required illumination and neutralization by the therapist so that the therapeutic lenses were not clouded. Another complex illuminated by the patient's accusations and challenges was in another direction and evoked another self/selfobject dyad particular to the therapist. The hostile accusations evoked a familiar childhood drama in which the challenges of his siblings resulted in the fighting, in those ancient times, that he believed necessary for his survival. Of course, behind the intense reactions on his part to challenges in childhood was a lack of certitude. Sibling rivalry does not exist in its intense forms when one has a feeling of self-certitude, an adequate endowment of endogenous self-worth. A sibling's challenges are not reacted to as a reflection of one's diminished self-worth if the caretaker's selfobject infusion of worth is adequate or if the mirroring is given to achievement rather than to weakness.

The therapist's composite responses to a particular patient reveal the results of a reentry into a private world of sensitivities and fears based on one's own developmental deficits. In an important sense, the therapist goes through a re-resolution of conflicts in each psychotherapy or psychoanalysis that extends over a lengthy period. Re-resolution is an appropriate description since total mastery over one's complexes is never possible.

Each therapy does indeed involve the re-solution of two transferences—the patient's and the therapist's—in sufficient detail so that the major symptoms are reduced and significant intrapsychic transformations have occurred.

At the end of this therapy, although the patient's accusations could still cause a heightening of tension, the intensity of the therapist's reactions was so reduced (as is usual in the termination phase) as not to constitute any impediment to the actual termination. Perhaps the absence or presence of intense reactivity constitutes a sign from the therapist's side of termination-readiness.

Informed by the working through of the various intrapsychic positions that were illuminated in this patient's termination period, the therapist could then go on to confront him with the meaning of his accusations: He wished to insist that the therapist harbored negative feelings toward him, and termination constituted rejection. Now both could "see" that he unconsciously wished to terminate his psychotherapy while still not free from his old (secure but depriving) way of doing life—he to "be" the deprived one, the therapist to "be" the rejecting, depriving one.

Case 2. Mr. T.H.

The following clinical material represents a familiar subjective reaction in those therapists who are not themselves elderly. It is an experience of uneasiness in reaction to the psychic difficulties experienced by older patients. It represents the difficulties in overcoming the barriers to being the psychological caretaker to those who represent the caretaker of one's past.

Mr. T.H.: Well, I'll tell you I'm having a hell of a time

with Marge. She just gets on her high horse and that's all there is to it. I get so upset, I don't want to do anything. I start to fret. She don't want to kiss me or nothin' during those times. Then she'll start on me! "You're such a tyrant. You just want your own way about everything. You get so stubborn, you're so rigid. I can't stand the way you always have to have your way"—and on and on. I try to reason with her. I tell her she's too upset, that she's got to see someone, but she won't listen to me. She'll just go on and on and on. I get beside myself. I'm 74, and for 48 years, whenever she gets into one of those times, I'm a goner. It used to be a lot worse when I couldn't control her drinking. She'd be off on a tear and that's all there would be for days on end. I used to be beside myself. She'd just kick me out, literally kick me out of the house. I didn't know where to go or what to do then. It's been better for the past several years. But when she gets into that mood and gets that look in her eyes, I'm a goner.

The patient was a 74-year-old executive who was in treatment for depression. Shortly after the psychotherapy began, he revealed the details of his relationship with his wife. As can be seen from the brief vignette, he had always pedestalized his wife, who did not offer him nurturance for his chronic depressed state, and he never asked her to be more responsive to him. The anguish he experienced in his dealings with her was never spoken of to her in the form of entreaties for help. His perduring complaints were that *she* was in disarray and he could not get her back into equilibrium.

The therapist found it jarring to hear and see this distinguished-looking and sounding man reveal this "weakness" and these "undignified" reactions. The fact of his being able to experience himself as "under her power," as he stated, and "when she's that way, I'm a goner" was unnerving.

Some of the therapist's experiences during the therapy represent those resistances that need to be overcome so that the patients can be afforded an appropriate therapeutic relationship to which they are entitled. They also represent the "civilian" type of responses of, for example, being deferential to or trying to be helpful to an aging person. For the therapist, they also represent the resistance to giving up the wish to maintain an aging person as a source of direction and mirroring and not as a patient with needs for empathically derived psychotherapeutic relief. The therapist in this case was required to investigate the particular selfobject transference need of the patient, which was to be seen as a dignified patriarch who could offer the therapist direction.

These considerations from the side of the therapist are vital to assisting aging patients in obtaining psychotherapeutic services.

Case 3. Ms. F.N.

Another type of reaction in therapists is that experienced when an aging patient is going through a psychological or physiological crisis or is in the process of dying.

During such times, the therapist is called on to maintain the posture of an empathic therapist and not to provide the unprofessional response of awe and immobilization so familiar to family members and friends of an aging person who is dying.

Ms. F.N.: (*whispering*) It's so good to see you. I didn't think you could come here to see me in this place (intensive care unit). I'm so tired. (*goes to sleep for a few minutes*) Oh, I'm sorry. This medicine cuts the pain but I just fall asleep. (*smiles*) It's so good to see you. (*falls back to sleep*)

The therapist's reaction was familiar to him. Each time he visited and worked with the dying, he would feel a sense of awe, as if he were in the presence of an event beyond his comprehension or ability to master. He found that he had to work to extricate himself from this reaction and to get back to his duties as the empathic psychotherapist and determine what posture he should be assuming toward this unique person. The therapist's reaction was based on his background of visiting aging or dying relatives and attending their funerals at an age when he could not comprehend the permanent separation experience of death. He also found this to be a reaction that he would revisit each time he worked with the dying, and each time, with less difficulty over the years, he would need to remove himself from this numinous experience.

Reactions to Deficits in the Patient

Finally, another reaction of which the therapist must be mindful is that of inadvertently patronizing the aging patient—a reaction familiar to those who work with aging people who find it difficult to get about or cannot hear well, or who show lapses in their cognitive skills. A very common form of patronizing is that shown when the therapist becomes jocular in reacting to one of the patient's deficits, such as the patient's forgetting the time of an appointment or not hearing correctly. All these forms of patronizing, including being too solicitous, may be regarded by the aged patient as unempathic and unhelpful since they are culturally derived platitudes rather than empathically derived attitudes. The patient with a hearing problem should not be helped to avoid or deny it, but should be seriously evalutated since the hearing loss may be amenable to the use of a hearing aid. Memory loss is also an important deficit to be taken seriously. Aged patients may feel ashamed of expressing their difficulties in remembering, which bars acquiring advice about handling the problem, as well as obtaining the mirroring of the respectful therapist who can inform them of the modal nature of their difficulties. The patient with locomotion difficulties may need more rather than less exercise or to use a cane, and simply to be made aware of the nature of the modal aging of the spinal chord, as the posterior spinal columns and cerebellar tracts in many older people deteriorate to the point of causing balancing difficulties.

In all these instances, the therapist, in viewing the

aging process in his or her patients, must be mindful not to assume an unempathic posture, a "civilian posture," toward these patients and thereby deprive them of their right to obtain the empathic relationships they require.

9

Epilogue

The intent in writing this book was primarily to encourage psychotherpists to accept older patients for psychotherapy of all types, without regarding age alone as an impediment. When elderly people realize that they will be accepted for psychotherapy, it is to be hoped that more of them will seek help for their psychological distresses. While there are encourageing signs in our culture at large and in our medical culture that the aged are not as rejected as they once were, as a group they have not yet been made welcome in many areas of society. It is true that more positions are open to the aged and that age alone (the number of years the person has lived) cannot be used legally to bar a person from applying for or maintaining a position, but the acceptance, admiration, or cherishing of the aged as a particular cohort of people is not yet in evidence. The aged have not been awarded a place in society that offers the acceptance and/or nurturance that people in other developmental phases of the life cycle have received. Adolescents, for example, have been acknowledged throughout the West as a defined group, even though this is a developmental stage as delineated by society, whereas the very existence of old age as a developmental phase in humankind has never been accepted.

Gerontophobia, or an irrational fear of the elderly, encompasses a wide variety of anxieties—including the fear of becoming ill and facing deterioration and death. Another fear is the fear that, in relating to the elderly as a caretaker, one will lose one's leaders—that is, becoming a caretaker finalizes one's loss of dependency (see Chapter 2).

What are the implications of the difficulties that elderly people have in obtaining treatment? Moreover, what are the special difficulties that therapists have in neutralizing or working through their own phobias and transferences? There are several issues involved. One is the myth of the elderly in our culture that is a potent instigator of the negative reactions of the caretakers. This myth takes its place along with other prevalent myths that determine the fate of those toward whom a particular myth is directed. Thus the myths about women, Jews, Blacks, Asians, and other Untouchables determine the safety or danger, the acceptance or avoidance, the hatred or affection that these groups can expect from their surround. The particular cultural myths concerning Blacks or women, however, do *not* imply that the self-internalizations of the myths proceed along similar lines and with similar intensity in the individual selves within the culture. In the instance of the myth of the aged, its elements include a view of the aged as contagious entities who infect those with whom they make contact with the toxins of enfeeblement, deterioration, illness, and death. Thus avoiding elderly persons or placing them in institutions away from the mainstream of any metropolis serves a protective or detoxifying function. Therefore, the task in obtaining more psychological help for elderly patients who require psychotherapy is to demystify and demythify the elderly as a group.

One major approach in the demythifying process is familiarization. This approach must proceed along legal, educational, and clinical lines. In medical and graduate schools, the curricula are being expanded to include the teaching of the physiology, pathology, psychology, and psychopathology of the aging. However, at present, clinical experiences with the aged are haphazard or nonexistent in most medical schools. In psychiatric residencies, it is rare to find a rotation devoted to the diagnosis and treatment of the somatic and mental ills of elderly patients. While familiarization is helpful, it of itself will not diminish the resistances toward contact with the elderly. In the supervision of psychotherapists, however, a good deal of desensitization can take place as therapists uncover and work through some of their fears of being infected with the toxins of the elderly. Clearly, though, the intensive working through that would totally free a person from the fear of death and dying cannot be obtained in *any* educational process.

Another technique that can be of service to the therapist in neutralizing the uneasiness of dealing with the elderly is the use of a model of observation, of diagnosis, and of therapy, such as offered in this book. When the therapist of the elderly applies a systematic approach to the observations that have to be made and to making an empathic and therapeutic diagnosis based on these observations, the therapist's uneasiness is much diminished.

And still another aid to mitigating this uneasiness is to stress the similarities between the psychotherapeutic treatment of the elderly and that of patients in other age groups. Psychotherapy is psychotherapy for all ages; the use of abstinence, confrontations, and interpretations is the same for all patients and therapists. Moreover, the elderly patient, as do all patients who have the potential for trust and self-observation, will form an alliance and will study with the therapist as the therapist offers confrontations and interpretations.

What has been assumed here is that psychotherapy is not attempted with many elderly patients—and further, that the motivation for not pursuing psychotherapy is *not* rational. It is also maintained that if psychotherapy, with or without tranquilizers or antidepressants, is initiated, it will usually be supportive psychotherapy, and not intensive psychotherapy or psychoanalysis.

These findings and notions (based on the author's experiences in supervision and other clinical experiences) reflect the biases of the caretakers of the elderly. The underlying essential element is the need to maintain a distance from the feared elderly patient, the carrier of the disease of deterioration and death.

The irrational fear of death and dying—thanatophobia—affects everyone to some degree. It always requires a large measure of denial (the psychic repudiation of the percept) and disavowal (the psychic repudiation of the meaning of the percept) to be kept out of consciousness and thus be unable to inspire anxiety. As the elderly carry the message of the eventual fate awaiting us all, those whose fear of dying is poorly contained through inadequate denial and disavowal will respond to them with actions of dismissal, avoidance, and other efforts to wall them off to prevent establishing contact. In this sense, the prejudices toward the elderly and the resulting difficulty in providing caretakers to help them to meet any of their needs, including that for psychotherapy, is a never-ending dilemma, one that will always require monitoring to ensure that these prejudices, and the actions they foster (demeaning, shunning), be kept to a minimum.

The author, having expressed his concern over the biases toward the elderly and his attempts to understand those biases, would go on to add that when the fears of the elderly are diminished sufficiently so that more contact and more caretaking can be effected, their psychological treatment will provide special rewards for those who perform these services. Those psychotherapists who work with the elderly not only derive gratification from being able, it is hoped, to effect a positive change in their patients' selves, but also experience a sense of personal joy in obtaining a measure of transference gratification for themselves—a revived experience of pleasing *their* caretakers from their past, a phenomenon rarely spoken of or even acknowledged by psychotherapists. The pleasurable feeling of pleasing one's parents here revisited can be acknowledged by all psychotherapists as partial payment for their endeavors on behalf of their elderly patients.

References

Abraham, K. (1924a). *Selected papers on psychoanalysis*. London: Hogarth Press.

Abraham, K. (1924b). The applicability of psychoanalytic treatment to patients at an advanced age. In *Selected papers on psychoanalysis*. London: Hogarth Press.

Alexander, F. (1930). *Psychoanalysis of the total personality*. New York: Nervous and Mental Disease Publishing Co.

Alexander, F.G., & French, T.M. (1946). *Psychoanalytic therapy: Principles and applications*. New York: Ronald Press.

Baldwin, R.C., & Jolley, D.T. (1986). The prognosis of depression in old age. *British Journal of Psychiatry, 149*, 574.

Basch, M. (1981). Selfobject disorders and psychoanalytic theory: A historical perspective. *Journal of the American Psychoanalytic Association, 29*, 337-351.

Beckett, S. (1947, 1972). The end game. In S. de Beauvoir (Ed.), *The coming of age*. New York: Putnam.

Berezin, M., & Cath, S. (1965). *Geriatric psychiatry, grief, loss and emotional disorders in the aging process*. New York: International Universities Press.

Bibring, E. (1953). Metapsychology of depression. In P. Greenacre (Ed.), *Affective disorders*. New York: International Universities Press.

Blazer, D. (1982). The epidemiology of late life in depression. *Journal of the American Geriatric Society, 30*, 587.

Boskin, M.J. (1986). *Too many promises: The uncertain future of social security*. Homewood, Illinois: Dow Jones-Irwin.

Brody, E. (1985). Parent care as a narrative family stress. *Gerontologist, 25*, 19.

Busse, E.W., & Pfeiffer, E. (1972). *Behavioral adaptation in late life*. Boston: Little Brown.

Butler, R.N. (1963). The life review: An interpretation of reminiscence in the aged. *Psychiatry, 26,* 65.
Butler, R.N. (1970). Looking forward to what? The life review, legacy and excessive identity versus change. *American Behavioral Scientist, 14,* 121-128.
Butler, R.N. (1975). *Why survive? Being old in America.* New York: Harper & Row.
Butler, R.N. (1978). Ageism: Another form of bigotry. In M. Seltzer, S.L. Corbett, & R. Atchley (Eds.), *Social problems of the aging.* Belmont, CA: Wadsworth.
Daniels, R. (1976). Manifestations of transference: Their implication for the first phase of psychoanalysis. *Journal of the American Psychoanalytic Association, 17,* 995-1014.
De Beauvoir, S. (Ed.) (1972). *The coming of age.* New York: Putnam.
Deutsch, F. (1949). *Applied psychoanalysis; Selected objectives of psychotherapy.* New York: Grune & Stratton.
Dewald, P. (1964). *Psychotherapy: A dynamic approach.* New York: Basic Books.
Erikson, E. (1959). Personal communication.
Erikson, E. (1982). *The life cycle completed,* New York: Norton.
Freud, S. (1898). Sexuality in the etiology of neurosis. In *Standard Edition* (vol. 3, pp. 261-287). London: Hogarth Press, 1962.
Freud, S. (1905). Fragments of an analysis of a case of hysteria. In *Standard Edition* (vol. 7, pp. 3-122). London: Hogarth Press, 1953.
Freud, S. (1906). On transience. In *Standard Edition* (vol. 7, p. 155). London: Hogarth Press, 1958.
Freud, S. (1912a). The dynamics of transference. In *Standard Edition* (vol. 12, pp. 97-108). London: Hogarth Press, 1958.
Freud, S. (1912b). Recommendations to physicians practicing psychoanalysis. In *Standard Edition* (vol. 12). London: Hogarth Press, 1958.
Freud, S. (1913). On beginning the treatment. In *Standard Edition* (vol. 12, pp. 121-144). London: Hogarth Press, 1958.
Freud, S. (1914). Remembering, repeating and working through. In *Standard Edition* (vol. 12, pp. 145-157). London: Hogarth Press, 1958.
Freud, S. (1915). Observations on transference-love. In *Standard Edition* (vol. 12, pp. 157-172). London: Hogarth Press, 1958.
Freud, S. (1917), Mourning and melancholia. In *Standard Edition* (vol. 14, pp. 237-259). London: Hogarth Press, 1958.
Freud, S. (1924). On psychotherapy. In *Collected Papers* (vol. 1, p. 258). London: Hogarth Press.
Gill, M.M. (1954). Psychoanalysis and exploratory psychotherapy. *Journal of the American Psychoanalytic Association, 2,* 771-797.

Ginzberg, R. (1950). Psychology in everyday geriatrics. *Geriatrics, 5,* 36-43.

Ginzberg, R. (1953). Geriatric ward psychiatry: Techniques in the psychological management of elderly psychotics. *American Journal of Psychiatry, 110,* 296-300.

Gitelson, M. (1948). The emotional problems of elderly people. *Geriatrics, 3,* 135-150.

Gitelson, M. (1952). The emotional position of the analyst in the psychoanalytic situation. *International Journal of Psychoanalysis, 33,* 1-10.

Goethe, J.W. (1828). Selige Sehnsucht. In *Goethe's Werke: Vollstandige Ausgabe letzter Hand* (vol. 5). Stuttgart: Cutta.

Goldfarb, A.I (1955). Psychotherapy of aged persons. IV. One aspect of the psychodynamics of the therapeutic situation with aged patients. *Psychoanalytic Review, 42,* 180-187.

Greenson, R. (1967). *The technique and practice of psychoanalysis* (vol. 1). New York: International Universities Press.

Greenspan, S.J. (1981). The influence of infantile trauma on genetic patterns. In S. Furst (Ed.), *Psychic trauma.* New York: Basic Books.

Grotjahn, M. (1955). Analytic psychotherapy with the elderly. *Psychoanalytic Review, 42,* 419-427.

Gutman, D. (1987). *Reclaimed powers.* New York: Basic Books.

Hiatt, H. (1971). Dynamic psychotherapy with the aging patient. *American Journal of Psychotherapy, 25,* 591-600.

Hiatt, H. (1972). Dynamic psychotherapy of the aged. *Current Psychiatric Therapies, 12,* 224-229.

Hollender, M.H. (1952). Individualizing the aged. *Social Casework, 33,* 337-342.

Jarvik, L. F., & Small, G.W. (1982). Issue on aging. *Psychiatric Clinics of North America, 5.*

Jelliffe, S.E. (1925). The old age factor in psychoanalytic therapy. *Medical Journal Rec., 121,* 7-12.

Kaufman, M.R. (1940). Old age and aging: The psychoanalytic point of view. *American Journal of Orthopsychiatry, 10,* 73-84.

Kohut, H. (1959). Introspection, empathy and psychoanalysis. *Journal of the American Psychoanalytic Association,* 459-483.

Kohut, H. (1966). Forms and transformations of narcissism. *Journal of the American Psychoanalytic Association, 14,* 243-273.

Kohut, H. (1971). *Analysis of the self.* New York: International Universities Press.

Kohut, H. (1977). *The restoration of the self.* New York: International Universities Press.

Kohut, H., & Wolf, E. (1978). The disorders of the self and their treatment. *International Journal of Psycho-Analysis, 59,* 413-425.

Levinson, D.J., with Darrow, C.N., Klein, E.B., Levinson, M.H., McKee, B. (1978). *The Seasons of a Man's Life*. New York: Alfred A. Knopf.

Levinson D.J. (1991). Personal communication.

Levinson D.J. (1976). Middle adulthood in modern society: A socio-psychological view. In: G. DiRenzo (Ed.), *Social character and social change*. Westport, CT: Greenwood Press.

Mechanic, D. (1972). Social psychological factors affecting the presentation of bodily complaints. *New England Journal of Medicine, 286*, 1132.

Meerloo, J.A.M. (1951). Contribution of psychoanalysis to the problem of the aged. In M. Heiman (Ed.), *Psychoanalysis and social work*. New York: International Universities Press.

Meerloo, J.A.M. (1955). Transference and resistance in geriatric psychotherapy. *Psychoanalytic Review, 42* 72-82.

Muslin, H. (1974). Clinical exercises in empathy. *Diseases of the Nervous System, 6*, 384-387.

Muslin, H. (1981). King Lear: Images of the self in old age. *Journal of Mental Imagery, 5*, 143-156.

Muslin, H. (1985). Beyond the pleasure principle. In J. Reppen (Ed.), *Beyond Freud: A study of modern psychoanalytic theorists*. Hillsdale, NJ: Erlbaum.

Muslin, H., & Clarke, S. (1988). Transference of the therapist of the elderly. *Journal of the American Academy of Psychoanalysis, 16*, 295-315.

Muslin, H., & Desai, P. (1985). Mahatma Gandhi. In C. Strozier & D. Offer (Eds.), *The leader*. New York: Plenum Press.

Muslin, H., & Epstein, L. (1980). Preliminary remarks on the rationale for psychotherapy of the aged. *Comprehensive Psychiatry, 21*, 1-12.

Muslin, H., & Gill, M. (1978). Transference in the Dora case. *Journal of the American Psychoanalytic Association, 26*, 311-328.

Muslin, H., & Jobe, T. (1991). *Lyndon Johnson: The Tragic Self*. New York: Plenum Press.

Muslin, H., & Val, E. (1987). *The psychotherapy of the self*. New York: Brunner/Mazel.

Neugarten, B. (1964). *Personality and later life*. New York: Atherton.

Neugarten, B., Havighurst, R., & Tobin, S. (1968). *Middle age and aging: A reader in social psychology*. Chicago: University of Chicago Press.

Oberleder, M. (1970). Crisis therapy in mental breakdown of the aging. *Gerontologist, 10*, 111-114.

Peck, A. (1966). Psychotherapy of the aged. *Journal of the American Geriatric Society, 14*, 748-753.

Piers, G., & Singer, M.B. (1953). *Shame and guilt.* Springfield, IL: Charles C. Thomas.

Pollock, G.H. (1987). The mourning liberation process: Ideas on the inner life of the older adult. In Sadavoy, J., Leszcz, M. (Eds.), *Treating the elderly with psychotherapy.* New York: International Universities Press.

Racker, H. (1957). The meanings and uses of countertransference. *Psychoanalytic Quarterly, 26,* 303-357.

Reich, A. (1960). Pathologic forms of self-esteem regulations. In *Psychoanalytic contributions.* New York: International Universities Press.

Riesman, D. (1954). Some clinical and cultural aspects of aging. *American Journal of Sociology, 59,* 379-383.

Rivlin, A.M., & Wiener, J.M. (1988). *Caring for the disabled elderly: Who will pay?* Washington, D.C.: Brooking Institution.

Rodin, J. (1986). Aging and health: Effects of the sense of control. *Science. 233,* 1271-1276.

Roth, M. (1976). The psychiatric disorders of later life. *Psychiatric Annals, 6,* 417.

Safirstein, S. (1972). Psychotherapy for geriatric patients. *New York State Medical Journal, 72,* 2743-2748.

Sanders, L.W. (1964). Adaptive relationship in early mother-child interaction. *Journal of the American Academy of Child Psychology, 3,* 231-264.

Sandler, A.M. (1978). Problem in the psychoanalysis of an aging narcissistic patient. *Geriatric Psychoanalysis,* 11:5-36.

Schlessinger, N., & Robbins, F. (1983). *A developmental view of the psychoanalytic process.* New York: International Universities Press.

Schur, M. (1972). *Freud: Living and dying.* New York: International Universities Press.

Shakespeare, W. (1952). *King Lear.* Arden edition. New York: Methuen Press.

Shakespeare, W. (1952). *As You Like It.* Arden Edition. New York: Methuen Press.

Sheps, J. (1955). Psychotherapy of the neurotic aged. *Journal of Chronic Diseases, 2,* 282-286.

Sophocles (1942). Introduction to Philoctetes. In D. Greene & R. Lattimore (Eds.), *The complete Greek tragedy.* Chicago: University of Chicago Press.

Stern, D. (1984). *The interpersonal world of the infant.* New York: Basic Books.

Swift, J. (1952), *Gulliver's travels.* In *Great books* (vol. 36). Chicago: Encyclopaedia Brittanica.

Tarachow, S. (1963). An introduction to psychotherapy. New York: International Universities Press.

Tolpin, M. (1971). On the beginning of a cohesive self. Psychoanalytic Study of the Child, 26, 316-352.

Tolpin, M. (1978). Selfobjects and oedipal objects: A crucial development distinction. Psychoanalytic Study of the Child, 33, 167-187.

Tower, L. (1956). Countertransference. Journal of the American Psychoanalytic Association, 4, 224-255.

Wayne, G.J. (1953). Modified psychoanalytic therapy in senescence. Psychoanalytic Review, 40, 99-116.

Weinberg, J. (1951). Psychiatric techniques in the treatment of older people. In W. Donahue & C. Tibbitts (Eds.), Growing in the older years. Ann Arbor, MI: University of Michigan Press.

Wolf, E. (1980). On the developmental line of selfobject relations. In A. Goldberg (Ed.), Advances in self psychology. New York: International Universities Press.

Zinberg, N.E. (1964). Psychoanalytic consideration of aging. Journal of the American Psychoanalytic Association, 12, 151-159.

Zinberg, N. & Kaufman, I. (1963). Normal psychology of the aging process. New York: International Universities Press.

Zola, E. (1972). La terre. In S. de Beauvoir (Ed.), The coming of age. New York: Putnam.